Backfire

Kennedy Seagrave

Archway Publishing books may be ordered through booksellers or by contacting:

Archway Publishing
1663 Liberty Drive
Bloomington, IN 47403
www.archwaypublishing.com
1 (888) 242-5904

ISBN: 978-1-4808-6370-5 (sc)
ISBN: 978-1-4808-6369-9 (e)

Library of Congress Control Number: 2018946707

Print information available on the last page.

Archway Publishing rev. date: 6/12/2018

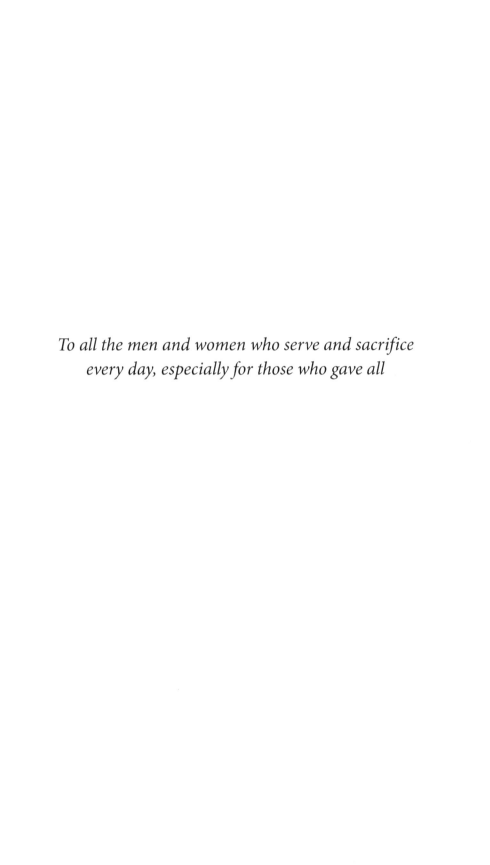

To all the men and women who serve and sacrifice every day, especially for those who gave all

Contents

INTRODUCTION IX

CHAPTER ONE 1
Size-Up

CHAPTER TWO.. 11
Identifying Safety Hazards

CHAPTER 3 12
Offensive versus Defensive Attack

CHAPTER FOUR 14
Incident Command and Control

CHAPTER FIVE.. 18
Strategy

CHAPTER SIX 31
Risk-Benefit Analysis

CHAPTER SEVEN.. 53
Escape Plan

CHAPTER EIGHT 68
Preplan

CHAPTER NINE 82
Communications

CHAPTER TEN 98
360 Walk Around

CHAPTER ELEVEN 119
Protect Exposures

CHAPTER TWELVE... 137
Fire Control

CHAPTER THIRTEEN 151
Fully Involved

CHAPTER FOURTEEN.. 156
Mayday

CHAPTER FIFTEEN 165
Fire Out

CHAPTER SIXTEEN 175
PIA

Introduction

I'm a retired fire battalion chief of a metro-sized department. Although I moved frequently growing up because my father was in the military, he settled on retiring in a military town, as did his father before him. While the area has a large military presence, it also has another large transient population of tourists because it is a coastal town. I started my career in the fire service as a newlywed, but this and other things would change in my personal life as well. At the time, my new husband owned a gym and managed a family-owned restaurant.

When I retired, I wrote down my feelings about my fire service career. I had mixed feelings about my fire service experience. I certainly didn't think that after all the effort and struggle to succeed as a female in the fire service it would end so unceremoniously. Part of the way I retired was by choice, but what did it all really mean? Why had I put myself through it, and what could I learn from it?

I felt like there had to be a bigger purpose than to just make it to a retirement date. I had lived and breathed the fire service. It was like running a race but with no one at the finish line to cheer me on or reward me for finishing the race.

That realization caused me to become angry, so I started writing down my frustrations, just to get what I felt was the frustration of the experience out of my system. I felt better but not satisfied. I started to see patterns and have realizations. I'd lived the fire service long enough to know that it had become part of who I was and how I approached everyday life.

My roommate after high school was dating a firefighter. She liked the idea of his shift work schedule. The schedule was twenty-four hours on duty and forty-eight hours off duty. What attracted her most to the job was the shift schedule, which equated to only working ten days a month. She asked me to apply to the fire department with her. She would end up not progressing through the fire department hiring process, but she successfully completed the police department's hiring process and became a police officer.

Little did I know that my decision to apply and go through the fire department's hiring process would change my life.

This process spread out over a year between the time I applied and when I was made an offer for employment. The first step was a written exam, then a physical-agility test, followed by a background check that included a criminal-history report. Nothing criminal was found in my background investigation, so my interview was scheduled. That went well, so a polygraph test and psychiatric evaluation were completed.

I didn't really give the process much thought at first. It was only a response to a friend's request to go through the hiring process and support her. The steps in the process were spread out far enough that they didn't occupy my conscious thoughts. I was working a regular nine-to-five job. I worked out at the gym and worked at the restaurant my soon-to-be husband owned that kept me busy on nights and weekends.

I was in good shape. I was young and doing some bodybuilding. I didn't know what the physical-agility entrance exam for a firefighter entailed, but I figured I was young and strong enough to just show up and take it. On the day of the test, I remember I attracted some interest from the test proctors because I was able to complete the required pull-ups. I was amused because at the time I could do more. I thought it funny that they were so easily impressed. At each phase of the test I excelled, and I didn't find the tasks to be difficult.

Because I had stood out at the pull-up station, more proctors appeared interested in how I'd do at each stage of the test. There was great excitement when I could drag the dummy a hundred feet while wearing the breathing apparatus. I was surprised I didn't have to do more with the mannequin.

One day after my roommate and I had applied with the fire department, I came home and experienced quite a scare. No one was home. When I opened the door, I saw what looked like a black man asleep on the living room floor. My heart stopped. I figured he'd somehow gotten in the house through an open window. A door leading to the porch from the kitchen was also routinely left unlocked. I thought perhaps he was homeless and looking for a place to sleep. There was a large transient homeless population at the beach where the house was located. So that was my initial impression of what had happened. I looked from the doorway more closely and realized it wasn't a living person.

It took a minute for me to figure out it was a mannequin burned black from fire and smoke, but I'd had no idea my roommate's boyfriend had brought it over to help her prepare for the physical-agility test.

Once I got over the shock, I picked up the mannequin and carried it up the stairs of our two-story house. I was curious if I was capable of doing it. I didn't know how much the mannequin weighed, but I was able to perform the task. On the day of the physical-agility test, I was only required to drag the mannequin. It was easy. I had assumed I would have to carry it for the physical entrance exam.

I received an interview that was scheduled the day after I returned home from my honeymoon. I was quite relaxed and, up to this point, had really only continued in the process because I didn't have a reason not to. I had no conflicts with the scheduled dates for the steps in the process, but I lacked commitment and the desire to become a firefighter. If my interview had been scheduled during my honeymoon, I wouldn't have shown up for it.

Later I would realize that my original interview took place in a conference room at fire headquarters where a panel of three white males took turns asking me questions with a female human resource department employee also in attendance. I only remember a few of the interview questions, but one question I do remember was what I thought the job of firefighter entailed. Because I had not committed to accept a position if offered one, I jokingly said I knew they cleaned a lot of toilets. Besides the obvious functions one would assume a firefighter did, that is the only thing I had ever heard my roommate's boyfriend talk about. He said the start of every shift began with a morning cleanup of the station. So that is the first thing that came out of my mouth. This response brought laughter from the board of interviewers.

Miraculously, I did well in the interview. Looking back, I am sure my offer of employment had more to do with fulfilling some sort of female and minority quota since there were few of either one at the time. I was scheduled for the next phase of the process, which was the polygraph test. I had never taken a polygraph test. I answered all the questions truthfully. I had no reason to lie, and I always tried to tell the truth, so I wasn't nervous about taking the test. The topics included questions about stealing and whether I took drugs. I knew I had answered the questions truthfully, but the test administrator seemed aggravated for some reason. He appeared to not believe me.

I guess he couldn't believe I hadn't done any of the things asked. He seemed to be using some sort of intimidation technique. He told me he didn't believe me and said he knew I was lying about something. I thought his behavior was irrational, and I was growing weary of his follow-up questions. The actual polygraph test had concluded.

I became impatient with his questioning and told him he was right. I told him I had punched a hole in my brother's ball when I was eight because mine had gone flat and I was jealous my brother still had his. I told him I had denied doing it when asked and hadn't told my parents about it until years later. I was feeling guilty and needed to confess. He was furious at this point, but I didn't care, because I still didn't really care if I got the job or not.

I passed the polygraph test.

When they called and offered me a job, I still hadn't had a serious conversation with my husband about the position. He knew I had been going through the process, but there had been no serious discussion about the possibility of being offered a job. He didn't offer much input during the discussion, so I led the conversation. Neither the restaurant nor gym business he owned was doing much more than paying the expenses to run.

A job with the city would come with benefits to include health insurance, which neither of us had. The final consideration was that the schedule only demanded ten days a month. I would still be able to fulfill my other obligations helping at the restaurant. My rationale was that I would have more to time at the restaurant because my current work schedule required me to work every day of the week. The ten-day-a-month schedule would allow me more time to work at the restaurant.

I evaluated the role of a firefighter. To me, a firefighter is someone who is selfless and willing to risk his or her life to help another. I liked the idea of being able to be in a position to help someone else. The ability to be able to make a positive difference in someone else's life appealed to me. I accepted the position with the fire department based on these reasons.

Both of my husband's businesses continued to do poorly, so my salary from the fire department was what we lived on. I now had to formalize a new plan on how this job would fit into my life goals and plans. I needed to conduct a size-up.

I have come to realize that small decisions made correctly have made all the difference in my life. The procedures utilized by fire professionals who specialize in public safety can also work well in helping everyday people make big decisions in their lives. They have helped me immensely during those times I had to make crucial choices in my own life. Identifying the significance of the choices was essential. Embracing a size-up outlook required me to disregard the often overpowering distractions and evaluate the situation before I made a decision to enter a burning building to save a life or even decided which college to attend. The size-up formula ensured I made evaluations of the situation before a choice was made.

I spent over twenty-six years in the fire department. I went into the fire service with limited knowledge of what the fire service was really all about. I didn't really think through my decision to join the fire service. It was one that had more to do with circumstance. Those decisions early on went on to make a large impact on the type of person I would become.

When I was still in high school, my goal during senior year was to carry a higher class load to fulfill the requirements to graduate early. My strategy was to achieve straight As to further my argument to be allowed to graduate.

I had strategically taken enough credits to graduate from high school with honors because of my early-graduation goal. I did this because my father was going to retire from the military during my junior year in high school.

I didn't attend my high school graduation or prom. I never had an expectation of living in the same house and keeping the same friends throughout my childhood growing up. I did, however, expect to be treated with fairness and respect. I believe every person has the same desires. I had a keen sense of fairness as I had experienced unfairness growing up.

Fairness and equity lessons were key to forming my value system, which helped me develop strong convictions such as equity, which is being fair to myself and to others. I recall an incident that reveals a depth of strength I didn't know existed.

While playing at school one day, an older boy and his friend approached and tried to intimidate me off a tetherball court when I had arrived first. He provided no justification for demanding that I give him the court other than he wanted it. I was determined not to let him have the court because I knew it wasn't fair. The fact that he was older didn't intimidate me.

The boy was angry because I told him I wasn't moving off the court. He slapped me across the face. I instantly slapped him back. He slapped me again, and I returned his slap.

This went back and forth several times.

A teacher saw the exchange and broke us up. I wasn't scared; I was infuriated. I was determined to stand my stand my ground and keep the tetherball court. It wasn't fair to myself to do otherwise. I fought for equality and felt justified doing so.

Unfair treatment in the fire service was just something I had already experienced in my real-life experiences. Injustice or unfairness was not a new concept for me that I had to learn to overcome or deal with. It was already a part of my life experiences, so it was easier to accept or navigate around.

Maybe these realizations and what I learned in the fire service could help someone else. I hope you find some of my life lessons using fire terminology to be beneficial in your life. So let's get started and conduct our first size-up!

CHAPTER ONE

Size-Up

A size-up in the fire department is conducted on every emergency incident. It starts with the initial call for service. A size-up is important to ensure firefighter safety in an emergency. Size-ups include many things, such as firefighter's initial impressions, how long a fire has been burning, type of occupancy, and the situation found upon his or her arrival. Walking completely around a structure is important to get the whole picture during a size-up.

A size-up can be conducted in any situation. It doesn't take long, and the more you conduct them, the quicker you become in conducting them. If you set up a routine of conducting size-ups, they can be done effortlessly, naturally, and automatically. You can start making observations as soon as you learn about a problem. The steps in your size-ups of situations can become routine and effortless.

Size-ups are the simple yet effective formulas firefighters use each time they arrive at emergency scenes. Here is my first size-up of fires.

I suffered a burn injury in recruit training. It was the last fire burn evolution of the academy. A burn evolution assesses certain skills during a fire, and those skills are accomplished in a logical order. At the time, not all burns were conducted at the training-center burn building. The training staff had obtained an abandoned structure to conduct the last live-burn evolution. It was conducted in one of the abandoned barracks on one of the local army bases.

The building was large wood-truss construction. Leftover jet fuel was used as an accelerant to start the fire. The fire instructors had found it in the storage barracks given to us to burn. Accelerants increased the volume of fire to enhance the fire volume during our fire recruit academy's last burn.

Instructors nailed the door shut, which was already held in place by a large wooden slat that covered both wooden doors that swung in. Instructors chose to operate from a thousand-gallon tanker on location as their one and only source of water. Today, two are required. Generally, tankers are only used as emergency backup water supplies. This is only after a constant water source is secured, preferably through a fire hydrant. Nailing doors shut, lack of water supply, and using accelerants are not safe practices when conducting live-fire burns by today's standards.

The fire was through the roof as our crew entered the structure. This information was never communicated to inside crews, and the instructors didn't stop the fire evolution. The fire was already compromising the integrity of the roof structure because of its wooden-truss construction, which experience early collapse in fires.

It had taken a long time to make entry due to the additional efforts to block the one and only egress. The fire load was large because there were contents inside that included mattresses and furniture. Only ordinary material like wood and straw are used today. The additional fire load, the added accelerant, the blocked egress, and lack of a water supply added up to a recipe for disaster. Any one of these items was grounds to stop a fire evolution. Instead, there were jeers to get inside. They had built a special fire for us.

When my crew was about forty feet inside of an approximately one-hundred-foot-long building, the fire flashed on and over us. A flashover occurs when burning materials during the burning process put off gas that ignites upon reaching its ignition temperature. The result is a violent, sudden all-encompassing ignition of this gas. It's hard if not impossible to escape the effects of the intense heat.

Prior to this time, there had been high heat, heavy black smoke, and no visibility. Sudden high heat is an indication of an impending flashover. Flashovers were covered in the textbook during the school, but there is no lesson better than personal experience. I remember thinking that the fire seemed pretty hot and perhaps this must be the kind of heat the book was talking about, but I had not experienced this hot a fire before.

Even though there was a large volume of fire coming from the roof, our crew entered the compromised structure. There is a certain level of fear that an instructor instills in recruits. In my case, the instructors were the ones who could either pass or fail me in the recruit school. They were the obstacle to overcome to graduate. I deferred to their professional expertise since I had no prior firefighting knowledge.

Our crew encountered thick, black smoke due to the extra materials burning and the added accelerant.

The crew dared not complain it was too hot as this was part of our rite of passage to take the heat. This was reinforced and communicated again to us by the jostling and comments that the instructors had prepared a special fire for us. The instructors repeated the order for our crew to get in there.

After our entry, when our crew tried to use the hose line, there was no water pressure. What little water there had been was used quickly by outside crews who had tried to douse the intense flames that were visible from the outside.

Our interior crew lost water pressure because crews outside used the water to try to put some of the flames out. Water is normally not directed toward interior crews. It creates steam conversion and results in steam burns, but they had done it as a last resort.

Our crew wasn't receiving any radio communications. There was only one radio for our crew, and I didn't have possession of it. It was strange to me that I didn't hear any communications. My crew member tried to send a message, but there was no indication that his message wasn't sent.

The radios then were UHF, not the VHF type that firefighters have today. Now when you key a portable radio, there is a beep that indicates you've hit a radio signal repeater. The noise from the large fire load burning would have prevented hearing the sound the repeater makes anyway.

Crews all took turns in the front or lead of the hose line. The lead person took the radio. My position for this evolution was in the middle of our three-person crew. My initial assessment of not hearing any radio communications was that the instructors were intentionally not responding to our calls on the radio as they had left us on our own before in other training exercises.

The instructors had warned us before the last burn scenario that everyone could still flunk out of the academy if the evolution wasn't completed successfully. Their demeanor and attitude about insisting the crew make entry even under the high heat and amount of fire visible only confirmed to me their seriousness. The radios back then weren't as sophisticated and stopped working at high heat temperatures. Our crew had experienced similar intermittent problems with radio transmissions inside the burn building before. The concrete walls were thick.

I had experienced hot fires before. Large, hot fires were routinely built to separate the men from the boys during fire evolutions. It was another way to ensure fire recruits who left the academy could take the heat. Instructors taught you to face your fear and not retreat just because a fire was hot. While all this was unfolding inside, the instructors were outside yelling from the doorway. They didn't try to make entry and couldn't make contact with us. They weren't dressed in their personal protective gear for the evolution. Instructors today are the safeties to rescue firefighters experiencing difficulty during training evolutions. But back then it wasn't a requirement to have an instructor with fire recruits. Our crew couldn't hear the instructors calling us from the door. The sounds of the heavily involved fire producing a crackling and popping of the added combustibles burning, along with an actual roaring sound due to the large volume of fire prevented us from hearing them. Our crew was in trouble and needed help. Someone should have called a Mayday.

Firefighters call Maydays when they are lost, disoriented, trapped, or running low on air and can't exit a structure without assistance. It causes great anxiety to hear a firefighter make a call on the radio for a Mayday. Firefighters hesitate to call them or usually wait too long, but a Mayday can save their lives.

Going to locate a downed firefighter may require finding another means of egress as the way the firefighter entered has been compromised.

I finally decided the fire was getting too hot during the recruit burn evolution, but an imperative rule of firefighting is that you never leave a fellow firefighter behind. In a recruit academy, you form a bond with other fire recruits in your class. When I turned to look back to check on the location and welfare of the crew member behind me, there was zero visibility.

I couldn't see that firefighter, and I became aware that the sound of breathing through the breathing apparatus could no longer be heard from the crewmate behind me. The sound of breathing through a regulator makes a distinct sound, and I could only faintly hear it. It was alarming that it sounded so far behind me. I turned back to try to communicate this to the lead member of our crew. I had been dragging hose and advancing it in the building as the location of the fire was being located. It was then that the hose line kinked in my hand. The realization hit me that water pressure was lost.

I faced a personal dilemma in going back to check on the missing crew member behind me because it meant leaving the one in front of me alone. I considered the firefighter positioned behind me to be in a less dangerous position than the one in front of me. The firefighter in front of me was closer to the fire and further from the door. I moved forward to communicate that contact had been lost with our crew member behind us.

On the way up the hose line, the risk factors were starting to add up. They included not having radio communications, not having all crew members with us, not having enough water, and the rapid increase in heat. These factors together equaled retreat. This was still a difficult decision because the seat of the fire hadn't been located and no water had been flowed. Our crew would have to face the consequences of exiting without having put out the fire. We had been the first in; we were supposed to be an example to the other firefighters who would come in behind us.

When I reached my crew member, he was frustrated and anxious because he was unable to locate the fire. It was hard to clearly communicate above the roar of the fire, even though we were screaming into each other's ears. I tried to tell him that there was no water pressure and we had lost one of our crew down the hose line somewhere. He confirmed he wasn't getting any radio communications.

He wasn't convinced water pressure had been lost until he tried to flow some water in front of us. He was determined to try to reach the fire but was unsure how much further that might be. Access to the interior of the structure had not been allowed prior to the fire, so it was hard to determine the interior layout.

When he couldn't get any water out of the hose, he considered my argument to exit. It was taking him longer to decide it was the right thing to do. I had already decided to leave but didn't feel like I could leave without him. That was not an option in my mind. I had already lost track of the crew member behind me. I knew where this member of our team was because we were having a conversation about retreating. To come out without a crew member was something you just did not do. There was verbal and physical punishment if you became separated from your crew. If you left someone behind during burn evolutions in recruit school, it was grounds for dismissal as a lack of team integrity meant failure and termination from the academy.

I was very concerned about the lack of water pressure, poor visibility, high heat, and lack of radio communications, but I was more afraid of losing a member of my crew. I remember feeling an overwhelming responsibility for my brother firefighter. As grave as I felt the current conditions were becoming, I couldn't compel myself to leave a fellow firefighter.

The only tool available to me was the power of persuasion. It was difficult to deliver the message due to the environment it was being delivered in. My teammate was determined to proceed. He had prior volunteer experience that had convinced me in prior situations to concede to his judgment, but conditions were deteriorating, and our efforts were ineffective. It was apparent to me that our efforts were in vain.

Firefighters crawl to avoid high heat, and that was now driving us to our bellies. We hadn't found the seat of the fire, but we had to get out of the building. The air being delivered from the air bottle through my regulator was so hot it was searing my lungs. It was painful, and I could actually feel air inhaled travel through the bronchial branches of my lungs. To breathe was painful, so I was trying to only breathe when absolutely necessary.

The heat was increasing, there was no visibility, radio communications couldn't be established, the water supply had been lost, and a team member was missing. The conditions were perfect for a flashover.

Flashovers are sudden and violent, but they can be predicted. The sudden rise of heat and flame patterns can help predict flashovers. There are real situations where environments can quickly get out of control, but just like flashovers, they can be predicted. The likelihood of their occurrence and your ability to identify them can have lasting consequences.

Before we reached the exit, the fire flashed over on us. That was all the convincing my crewmate needed. At that point, it was a matter of survival. All reason and prior plans were abandoned as a frantic effort for our personal safety and survival became the priority.

When the room flashed, I stood up and ran full speed toward the back of the building. I hit the wall so hard it knocked me off my feet and bounced me a few feet back. That's the first time I could see the light of the doorway and headed for it. Thankfully, I saw my brother firefighter who had been with me at the end of the hose line closest to the fire going out the door.

I had to wait for him to get out of the way. I almost crawled over him. It wasn't until I could see him crawling out the opening of the door that I considered his welfare again. When I saw the light coming from the outside, I knew I was going to survive.

Our helmet and shields were melted and dripping down as we rolled out the door. All the reflective tape on our coats was burning. Water cans off the fire engine were used to extinguish the flames on our coats by crews outside since there was no water left in the hose.

My gloves were so hot they were burning my skin as the interior material made contact with my hands. I flung the gloves off as I rolled out. They had gotten wet from water leaking out from the fire connections that extend the hose line, and I was receiving steam burns from them. A firefighter's gear has several layers, and each provides a function. The gear is designed to have a gap or air pocket to provide for more cooling. Each time my coat and pants touched me I received a compression burn.

I should have left my gloves on. My coat was so hot that when I went to touch the metal clips to take the coat off, the clips were too hot to touch. Every time the material of the coat touched my skin, it left another compression burn. I was desperate to get the coat off, and I felt like tearing it off at the seams.

When we stripped out of our gear, there was steam conversion off our bodies because the outside air was cooler than our bodies. Steam rolled off our skin, as we had been closer to the fire and spent the most time inside. Both of us looked sunburned.

I had not been able to do more than save myself on this incident, but I started to develop that sense of sacrifice when I stayed with a brother firefighter that day against all reason.

I had the help and motivation of the fear of dismissal from the academy to help me be committed to finding and extinguishing this fire.

There was fear of failure if the fire wasn't located and extinguished. That goal wasn't attainable, but it was still a factor in the delay of our retreat. I felt there were lessons to learn that needed to be evaluated after this event. The key events leading up to the near-miss fire fatality needed to be evaluated and critiqued so they wouldn't be repeated.

It was a perfect time for a postincident analysis (PIA).

A PIA, or after-action report, is an evaluation of what tactics went well and which didn't. Large-scale emergency incidents are evaluated afterward during a PIA. When there is an injury or near-miss accident, PIA helps identify those factors that contributed to the event so that the same mistakes aren't repeated. When an event results in an injury, the idea is to prevent a reoccurrence that could result in a fatality.

Evaluations are helpful in real life. I sometimes found myself repeating the same mistakes. I couldn't make corrections if I couldn't identify the repeating destructive patterns that led me back to the same place. So I had to identify the problem, address it, and make corrections. I also identified when something worked well. That way, I was able to repeat those behaviors or patterns that were effective and worked best in my life.

Through my personal experiences, my knowledge increased. This knowledge was cultivated through further training that resulted in wisdom. The intelligence gained through this process was what I relied on later in my career instead of fear.

The fear of failure in my recruit academy was a factor that altered my rational thought and judgment on the day of the burn. The training had been challenging and grueling. I had been able to identify the warning signs of high heat, poor visibility, lack of water, and no communications, but I had been in survival mode. I had been trying to survive the fire but also to survive the academy.

The inability to leave my teammate had been strong. I knew firsthand what the conditions were inside that structure. His personal safety had been at risk. He couldn't have survived the conditions.

The fear of failure and my concern for my brother firefighter had driven my decisions that day. I could have become one of the fire fatalities that occur every year in the fire service.

Later, it was determined that the crew member behind me who we had lost contact with had stayed by the door because it was so hot and there had been no visibility. Our crew integrity had failed at this point. The time spent inside the structure had only lasted a few minutes. Fatal errors can occur that fast.

A breakdown in communications had been a factor, which demonstrates how important clear communications can be. Had an effort been made to find our missing crew member, the exit would have been in view when the fire flashed, and our injuries wouldn't have been as severe.

At this point in my career, I had only mastered tasks. Fire recruits are not taught many tactical considerations. The information taught is limited to the knowledge required to extinguish fires and conduct searches. Fire-stream tactics are taught to help firefighters identify when a fog or a straight-stream fire attack should be used. A solid stream is used to penetrate a fire, and a fog stream is used to utilize steam conversion to extinguish a fire with less water.

A fog stream generally works best in a smaller confined area. The walls confine the water droplets of a fog stream to get good steam conversion to help extinguish a fire. Using a fog stream under the right conditions can lessen the likelihood of a flashover and reduces the heat in a structure.

The size of the structure, the amount of flames visible, the distance from them, and the intensity of the fire drove our decision to use a straight stream to extinguish the fire. Straight steams require more water. A straight stream is what outside crews used to try to get the extension to reach the fire and penetrate the large volume of fire.

Using a fog stream at the ceiling level would have cooled down the gases accumulating there and helped prevent the flashover. As recruits operating on limited knowledge and experience, it was a tactic unfamiliar to us and not considered.

The instructors failed by setting up a dangerous training fire scenario. They intentionally decreased our likelihood of success. I learned to respect fire. It was dangerous. It commanded focused attention. Complacency could kill.

Outside crews seemed relieved. Everyone thought we had already perished in the fire. Not long after we exited, the whole building became fully engulfed in flames, and the roof caved in. Their relief also stemmed from not having to make an entry themselves.

The first burn evolution became the last and only burn of the day. I received a burn on my face under my left eye that produced a blister and a scab. My face piece started to fail due to the intense heat, and the result was a radiant burn right through the lens because the lens had started to fail and melt. This also only occurs at high heat not conducive to interior firefighting.

The lens is rated to fail around three hundred and twenty-five degrees. Firefighting gear is good and protects firefighters from extreme types of heat. That is why it is so important you take care of it and wear it properly. The other firefighter inside with me had burns around his face where there was a gap between his face piece and his flash hood. Both of us had to be treated for burns.

Initially, the instructors discussed not taking us for medical treatment because that would require paperwork, a record of the injury, creating a paper trail that identifies that an event had happened, documentation that there had been an accident.

As my career progressed, I became more confident in fire behavior and the warning signs of flashover. Over time I was able to identify when conditions were tenable to attempt interior firefighting operations. This wisdom was gained through personal firsthand knowledge and experience. Outside influences would still continue to be strong factors in actual outcomes, however.

As time went on, I came to more fully realize when to ask for help or decide when I needed to get out of an untenable environment. It could be fatal to wait too long.

In the size-up of my burn injury, I realized that I couldn't entirely rely on the expertise of other people. Just because someone else had more experience in firefighting didn't mean he or she had better common sense or judgment. My personal safety was my responsibility. Sometimes I found myself in bad situations because of the bad decisions made by others. My skills needed to be good so I could rely on those skills to increase my chances of survival. I needed my own personal escape plan.

Firefighters should have an escape plan or other means of egress. It may be necessary to retreat for your safety and for the safety of others in your crew. If your efforts aren't effective, you may not have any other option but to retreat. If you have attempted many times to extinguish a fire and utilized all the options available to you, it may just be time to give up on a situation that has no hope of improving.

The gross neglect of instructors created a dangerous environment that required me to evacuate. Poor judgment and actions by those in authority to make decisions can set up a scenario for firefighter injury and death.

Things went wrong during my recruit fire because of the poor judgment and decisions made by the fire instructors. They lacked the courage to share what was learned from their mistakes.

After my burn was treated, I wanted to learn from the incident, and I started asking questions. The result was a personal assault from the instructors. I was verbally reprimanded for daring to question their decisions and judgment. They still determined whether I would graduate or not.

I realized not all policies and rules were enforced in the department. They existed, but they were not always followed or enforced. Sometimes you may have to switch from an offensive to a defensive attack.

CHAPTER TWO

Identifying Safety Hazards

Identifying safety hazards is the first thing firefighters are trained to look for. There were safety hazards to my reputation and firefighting abilities. There were also real physical safety hazards. That is why it is important to identify what safety hazards lay ahead of me. If I could preplan the threats, I could plan my strategy to ensure my safety.

Firefighters identify safety hazards before they proceed because they have to be in a position to still be effective and able to finish the task. If you are not aware of the hazards before you tackle an issue, you may become a casualty and never be in a position to address the problem. You could walk right into a hazardous situation without the proper protective equipment or resources you need.

My strategy was to establish my credibility in the fire service based on merit. The very beginning of my fire service career provided an example of poor moral character. It helped me decide what kind of leader that I eventually wanted to be. In my experience during the fire recruit academy, the people with power and authority lacked personal integrity. My strategy was to maneuver around their deficiency in character but to become a better leader myself.

I determined that a career in the fire service was worth taking some risks. I would, however, need a well-considered strategy to succeed. First, I needed to learn how to identify the safety hazards.

CHAPTER 3

Offensive versus Defensive Attack

Firefighters conduct proper size-ups to identify all the safety concerns so they can choose the proper fire attack. Then they can decide whether they should initiate an interior offensive attack or an exterior defensive attack. Factors to consider should include personal risk involved, readiness, and what the benefit will be to perform the attack.

I was grateful that we hadn't been more severely burned. Receiving brand-new turnout firefighting gear was just one of the small consequences. This was something that was joked about. During a recruit academy, you participate in many live burns. The condition of the gear is an outward symbol that you have experienced and fought the fire demon.

Our arrival in fire operations with brand-new gear fueled the distrust of operational personnel that we had never been introduced to fire even though I still had the evidence on my face.

No investigation was ever held about this near-miss fire training fatality. No changes were made to the way live burns were conducted. Later, as the chief of training, it became my priority to ensure safety briefings and guidelines were followed.

I learned the importance of personal protective equipment (PPE) and the need to keep it in top condition. It is more important that it is operational than to try to display the evidence of your exposure to the fire beast. You may need to rely on it in an emergency. But the culture in the fire service still exists that dirty gear is an outward sign of your experience in fighting fire.

Unspoken contests still exist today about who can stay in a fire the longest and endure the most heat. Intelligent firefighters have the wisdom to respect fires and know when it is time to get out. This experience did give me a barometer for the rest of my career of when a fire was too hot and it was time to get out. Getting burned is nothing to brag about.

This and other experiences proved that not everything was allowed to be discussed during after-action reports. The challenge was being able to determine what the inadmissible items were. Generally, they were the most important items to correct, but they weren't allowed to be discussed.

This would change later in my career when I gained more intelligence about my job and acquired confidence. Intimidation and being threatened were not effective deterrents throughout the progression of my career, but that didn't mean those tactics still weren't used on me.

The purpose of PIAs is to learn what operations worked well and which didn't. They were supposed to promote a safe learning environment. The ultimate goal was to provide the best service and ensure firefighter safety while doing it. The PIA's job was to identify problems that needed to be corrected and strategies that worked to encourage their use in future incidents.

Fear of failure and loss of financial stability were motivating factors that resulted in my poor judgment. There were outside factors that contributed to what went wrong. Those issues should have been identified and learned from so similar future events didn't occur. Unfortunately, a PIA was never conducted to correct this fires mistakes.

My personal integrity was tested early in my career. It appeared a choice had to be made between my success in the fire service and my personal integrity.

CHAPTER FOUR

Incident Command and Control

Set up a strong incident command system to ensure command and control of your incident. A strong leader to direct operations ensures all the necessary benchmarks are covered. You should assess what your influence is on a team. If someone is in charge or leading, he or she is in the best position to see all the working parts of the incident.

Orders can be confusing. Sometimes you have to rely on the expertise of others. Because I was a new fire recruit, I had limited fire-behavior knowledge. I had to rely on the expertise of the instructors. I didn't have enough experience or confidence to consider they may not have the required knowledge or expertise themselves.

Communications have to be correctly delivered and received to be effective. Be clear and concise. The priorities identified should be supported by the strategy. Your actions should support what you really want to achieve. Discipline is required of firefighters to follow strategic plans. I needed to evaluate my personal decisions to ensure my actions were taking me closer toward my goal.

Incident commanders have the most information to make the best decisions about what tactics should be used to support the overall strategy. I had the most information about what would work best for me to maintain control of my fire career.

I didn't have the wisdom and confidence yet to question instructors' authority or judgment in regard to fire behavior and attack, but I still had to make quick, accurate decisions that could result in errors. Some of these situations were not as physically threatening as a fire, but I could still get burned with consequences. Benchmarks provided regular assessments to check my progress.

The lessons I learned while gaining knowledge about the fire service actually helped me navigate through my career. I will explain more about what some of the fire terminology means since I use the lessons I learned from my acquired understanding of the fire service throughout my career and life.

I assessed the benchmarks of *fire under control* and *fire out* to assess my progress. It is important to keep fires under control. Then after the immediate threat of controlling the fire is handled, I could assess how to completely extinguish the fire.

How you control and extinguish fires will be different than how others do it. As you experience decision-making differences, you may find that not everyone shares the same value system when making decisions. Their values and what they prioritize will affect their decisions as they do yours.

The instructors fear of the burn being investigated motivated their continued poor judgment. Their mistakes would have become the subject of discussion, and that motivated them to continue to deny any wrongdoing. It was a defensive tactic and indirect. In this case, it wasn't followed up with an interior attack to fully extinguish the fire and identify the errors that resulted in this accident.

There was no extinguishment, so the cause of the fire couldn't be determined. Not everyone agrees with exterior defensive fire attacks, especially if there is no follow-up of an interior attack to ensure the fire is actually out. Without fire-cause determination, those types of fires can't be prevented in the future. No one wants to admit when they make a mistake. It is embarrassing and uncomfortable.

I had to take the time to do a size-up and be cautious while becoming educated on acceptable fire operations. Then I could be better prepared to fight the fires I was confronted with.

I had to acquire the wisdom required to properly identify safety hazards. With the wisdom, I was able to know how to develop a strong strategic plan and establish a strong incident command system. Checking for fire extension after a fire appears out will ensure there are no rekindles.

Don't be satisfied just because there are no longer flames visible. After a fire was out, I checked for the cause of the fire. It will give you an idea of how and where the fire started. You have to assess if the fire is really out. If you aren't willing to check for extension, the fire will present itself later even more intensely because it wasn't detected. Then the fire will only get bigger.

My personal after-action report identified that when someone in authority made a mistake, they were likely to take a defensive strategy and not admit the error. This created the same danger as firefighters not checking for hidden fires to make sure a fire is out. Their strategy was to downplay their error in tactical judgment. This limited the effectiveness of future live-fire evolutions. I determined that no fire origin and cause determination or rescue efforts were initiated.

I found that sometimes a primary search wasn't enough, and a more thorough secondary search needed to be completed.

Walking around the whole emergency scene gave me a clearer picture of the situation. On fire scenes, this is called a walk around, fast lap, or three sixty. This is where the gas and electricity is secured to limit those hazards during a fire.

There may be a need to open a window or door to ventilate a structure to improve the survivability for occupants. A threat to exposures or other nearby structures is evaluated during this firefighter walk around.

Every time there is a fire, the officer does a complete walk around even if it's a fast assessment to identify all the hazards. If firefighters don't walk all the way around a structure, they may miss someone hanging out the window, looking to be rescued. At the same time, after you stop your walk around to rescue that person, it is essential to complete the walk around so you don't you miss someone else in need of rescue.

Primary searches are rapid searches to save those in immediate danger. Secondary searches are more thorough after the immediate threat is mitigated. Primary searches are done simultaneously with fire attack. Secondary searches are more thorough and time consuming. Starting ventilation helps in the search for fire victims. I rarely found all the hidden casualties until I completed a secondary search.

Ventilation of smoke improves interior conditions for trapped or unconscious fire victims by introducing fresh air. It also improves the visibility for firefighters so they can more easily search for trapped or unconscious fire victims. Ventilation tactics improve the survivability of fire victims.

Ventilation practices worked for me. My goal was to reduce the toxic atmosphere so I could see a direction clearly to accomplish my goal. Some ventilation practices only work within narrow parameters and are time sensitive.

Don't be so focused on the main body of fire that you don't check the exposures nearby for fire extension.

Control exposures both interior and exterior as they can be affected by fire. Fire can spread to a nearby home. It can also spread inside a home in hidden spaces in the walls and progress to the attic.

During and after fires, threats to exposures or other nearby structures are evaluated. Initially, they are evaluated during the walk around. Even after a fire appears to be out, there are hidden spaces that need to be checked to ensure the fire is completely out and won't start again. These fires in hidden places can rekindle or reignite.

I identified some of the exposures encountered during incidents, but not all fire extension was identified early enough in my career. I would need to rely on a strong, well-thought-out strategy.

CHAPTER FIVE

Strategy

Strategy in the fire service is how you orchestrate tactics to achieve fire control, extinguishment, and rescue fire victims. Certain tasks need to be performed to support the tactics. Tasks are the specific steps required to perform the tactic. Tactics support the strategy, and tasks support the tactics.

Having this overall strategic plan would help me overcome struggles and challenges throughout my fire and personal life. I believe you can develop the skills and determination to excel and succeed in any environment. I acquired and developed skills throughout my life that helped me continuously adapt to many different situations and also paid big dividends both early and later in my professional career.

One strategy in the fire service is to provide fire control while there is a search for lost or trapped fire victims. A tactic used to support this strategy may be positive-pressure attack, which requires the specific placement of fans to provide a ventilation opening. The positive-pressure-attack tactic supports the overall strategy to find and locate trapped or lost fire victims.

Firefighters form a clear strategy before they commit resources to perform a tactic. Positive-pressure attack can be used before the fire attack to improve smoke conditions inside a structure, making it easier to search for lost or trapped occupants and also helping improve fire victim's chances of survivability. There were tactics and tasks to support the overall strategic plan.

Strategies to fight fires use tactics and assigns tasks that fit the overall strategic plan for protecting life and property.

I was able to fit into different environments in the fire department because of my experience of moving a lot. I believe my experiences growing up prepared me to be able to adapt and enabled me to accomplish hard things in the fire department.

Experiences in high school of not fitting into any particular group helped ground me and instill self-confidence and acceptance of who I was at the time. The experience of overcoming prejudice and not being included in groups helped me in my transition to a male-dominated profession. The fact that I was unwanted and not liked only made me more determined to succeed. I never wanted to just be a female quota in the fire service. I wanted to be included in the fire service. My operational assignment was at the first fire station for the city. The first building for the station had to be relocated in 1937 when a new truck was purchased that didn't fit in the building. The building I worked in was actually the site of a combination public safety office. When it first opened, the chief was over both the police and fire services when the city was just a town. The building had a back section that acted as the jail.

The building had a lot of history and character. When I worked there, the old jail was used as the gym for the station. There were many modifications to the original building to accommodate equipment that was purchased. The station had an old boiler system. In the winter, there was a loud banging noise as the hot water that flowed through the pipes of the radiator that expanded and tried to heat and keep up with the demand of the large open spaces.

I thought of the banging as the ghost of an old fireman from long ago. I thought about how he might be banging on the pipes to keep them working so the environment was pleasant for the firefighters on duty. It was rarely warm even with all the audible efforts of the ghost to warm the station.

I rarely rested with the combination of the noise of banging on the pipes and the anticipation of an emergency call. I was especially nervous as no one seemed receptive to teach me about fire behavior. It was clear from the first day my presence wasn't welcomed.

I was rewarded as I woke up to an alarm for a call in my sock feet to put on my turnout boots to step into a pool of water standing on the floor that had leaked from the radiator pipes. The boiler room itself was an old, creepy passageway to a rear bay of the station that housed an antique fire truck and utility vehicle. This bay was also where the washer and dryer were to wash uniforms. The only other way out of the bay was through the kitchen or through the bay door. The quickest and easiest way was through the dark closet of the boiler room. So you were forced to walk through that dark space where the ghost that banged on the pipes resided.

The pipes of the boiler and all other water pipes were exposed in the ceiling in the bays where the trucks sat ready to respond. The water that leaked from these pipes had old tape at the seams. They frequently leaked onto the fire trucks. The floors of the bay were painted. Daily cleanup required you to sweep and mop these floors after you got up the grease drippings from the trucks. Our daily practice was easier than routines of firefighters before us. They had to keep the floors painted, waxed, and buffed.

Another tradition was the fire pole that had to be polished and shined during the Saturday cleanup routine. The only thing that kept you from falling down its hole was two swinging doors. I had never seen one before, and I wasn't trained in its use. When a call came in at night, it was the quickest way to the truck. If you weren't competent in how to quickly mount the pole and quickly slide down it, the next firefighter would land on top of you at the bottom.

There was a mat that existed to lessen the jolt at the bottom. You knew it if your bladder was full, but there was no time for that if an emergency call had come in. The best practice was to squeeze the pole more tightly with your legs to slow yourself down. I eventually would learn how to competently use it over time with experience, but I wasn't comfortable using it at first.

I was sure that I would be in the way and trampled. I quickly took the stairs and walked around to the trucks in the beginning. Part of my avoiding the pole was that I would have to walk through the bunks of men to get to the pole. Since I was new, unsure, and lacked confidence yet, I was the first to jump up to get ready. They would be in various stages of dress. They had just been woken up and were in no mood for my uncertainty or timid approach of utilizing the pole to get to the truck.

Because of the circumstances I found myself in, I made sure I wasn't the last one to get dressed and be ready for a call. It helped that the radio dispatch system wiring was so old I could actually hear the call coming through the wire and hit the relay switch right before the bells went off and a call was dispatched. A loud bell and horn ensured no one slept through a call. I didn't want to bring any extra wrath or give anyone any reason to negatively notice me. I was busy trying to find my way.

The dayroom was furnished with donated couches and chairs made of stiff foam. Every time someone sat down, a puff of dirt and dust rose into the air. The room wasn't there for comfort but was a place to conduct desktop drills and have meetings and critiques of fires. At night, you could watch television. It wasn't really a comfortable place, but you could temporarily try to relax between calls for service. It might also become a restless place as everyone anticipated the next call for service.

The floor sagged and consisted of broken asbestos tiles that were still required to be waxed and buffed each Saturday worked. There was no other rationale or logic for doing it other than to continue the tradition of doing so. There was an old bell tower with an alarm that would be sounded to warn volunteer firefighters in years past to respond to the station for an emergency alarm. It was no longer in use and of ill repair. The structure leaked water that would make its way through the seams in the roof. Eventually, the structure rotted away from lack of maintenance and disuse.

This was the condition of my first assignment. Everyone at this historic fire station made such a fuss about me being assigned to work there in 1987, I couldn't imagine what the big deal was. On the surface, the place didn't look like it deserved such reverence. There were much newer stations with better living conditions I could have been assigned to. It was only after I realized its history that I could appreciate its significance.

I was the first women to be assigned to that station on that shift. When our recruit academy concluded and our assignments were announced, the saying spread that the first fire chief, who was deceased, was going to roll over in his grave that women were working at that station. I sized up right away that my presence wasn't going to be welcomed. I also knew that to succeed and survive I would have to do a good job and would have to rely on my own efforts.

Years later, I would come to realize it was the place my future father-in-law had started his career as one of the original firefighters hired. I arrived at that building in 1987, but that building was still held in time in 1937. All the ideals and perceptions of what a firefighter should be were still held strongly in place. It housed firemen not firefighters.

The station had two engines and one ladder company assigned there. This was the only station with three pieces of equipment in it. I was one of eight people assigned there. As the newest crew member, my assignment was to swing from the primary engine called the wagon to the second fire truck called the engine, depending on what type of call it was. The wagon responded to first-due fires. Fire stations are assigned a primary area of responsibility. A first due fire is a fire they are dispatched to in this area. If it was a call for emergency medical service (EMS), I would swing over to the engine.

Most of my first few years were a proving process. The other firefighters in the station made it clear I was not wanted at the fire station When I arrived at my assignment, there were stacks of *Playboy* magazines and posters laying around and hanging on locker doors. There was one big, open bunk room for everyone to sleep and shower in. The captain was the only one who had a private bathroom and bunkroom. I was allowed to use his private bath after he was finished instead of having to use the gang shower.

The male firefighters would walk naked by my bunk on the way back and forth to the shower. I received this as a strong message that they weren't going to change their routine. I concluded that if I wanted to stay there, I would have to adapt to the conditions. They weren't going to provide any special accommodations or make it comfortable for me.

I was intentionally left by myself while inside fighting fires, and crews would try to leave me behind and disorient me in the structure. Then they would critique my self-rescue out of the fire. All the undesirable assignments fell to me. New recruits were routinely given undesirable assignments. Probationary firefighters are given a lot of basic tasks to help orient them to station life and expose them to many different situations. I found success in being willing to take the assignments no one else wanted.

I gained experience and knowledge about many different things. In my early days at the station, they would send one person out in a utility vehicle to maintain the fire hydrants. During the time of greasing, painting, and ensuring there were no obstructions and water on the hydrants, I learned their locations. There were many fires where I was able to provide this information. When I started driving and needed to secure a water source, I knew where the hydrant was.

Another program I was assigned to complete was the prefire plan program. This program involved drawing structures and labeling where the fire connections and systems were along with the electrical shutoffs. While responding to these structures, I was more familiar with them and was able to navigate more easily in the interior. No one else wanted to do them. They sat and watched television or washed their personal vehicles while I drew prefire plans and provided the needed details to complete them. Few of these individuals were ever promoted. They never put forth any extra effort to be in positions to become promoted.

My size-up provided enough benchmarks to know I would have to be self-motivated and self-sufficient. This helped me overcome the physical and emotional challenges that presented themselves to me. It changed the amount of effort I put forth to excel at work.

Over time, I toughened up to the cruel things that were said and done to me. They did, however, create a growing insensitivity in me. An attitude of indifference grew because of the bad treatment I endured. The things I saw on emergency calls only reinforced my indifference. It was a self-preservation tactic.

The desire to keep my employment and the responsibility I felt to financially support my daughter outweighed any cruel behavior to deter me. A hard shell formed on the outside and pushed any hurt feelings or fear deep inside.

On shift, I was treated as one of the men and expected to perform like one. It was a test to see if I could perform the job or not. I didn't ask for help even if it was needed. I was hired to do the same job, so there was no reason to expect anything different. No one offered any help anyway. To ask for help or complain were not options in my mind.

The other shifts voiced the same attitudes when they relieved and were relieved by me. My relief wouldn't show up until the last possible moment. It is customary to relieve the off-going shift early to avoid them being caught on an emergency call and having to work over their shift. The shift I was relieving wouldn't take their gear off the truck and made comments that they felt it was their responsibility to ride the truck as long as possible to limit my lack of competence to the public on calls.

The captains on both the other shifts would undress me with their eyes and make derogatory statements. They would comment that they were glad I didn't work on their shift because it was a distraction. They would make specific comments about my private body parts and make offers of sex. Their crews mimicked the behavior.

I couldn't talk back to an officer, but I did to the other firefighters. I excelled in these verbal debates. Going for what hurt their egos was the most effective. It was out of character for me, but I was confronted with hostility.

Because you spent twenty-four hours together, many of the details of your private life were public knowledge. A married chief was sleeping with the wife of one of the firemen who worked for him. He controlled the fireman's leave, so it made it easy to track his location. The fireman figured out what was going on and left the station to catch them. He missed a call, and the truck had to respond short staffed to an incident. Some married captains would sleep at their girlfriend's house, and the truck would stop and pick them up on the way to calls.

Some firemen's wives and girlfriends would visit them at the station. When a wife called while they were on leave, another fireman would cover for him and tell her he was on a call. On occasion, both a fireman's wife and girlfriend would visit the station at the same time. The fireman's girlfriend would be snuck out of the station. Firemen would drink on duty or even come to work already drunk. This was the environment I worked in.

I survived in this environment in spite of the conditions. They actually did me a favor, making me become self-sufficient. The strategy based on my size-up was to work hard. My determination grew, and alternative methods were developed to get things done that were beyond my physical capacity to accomplish. This only made me stronger and more determined. The benefits were worth the risks.

It became a challenge to invent new ways to overcome obstacles. I learned to mount an external standpipe to the end of the aerial ladder by myself. This was a large, heavy, metal pipe that weighed around forty pounds. To get it to the tip of the ladder you had to walk along just the rungs of the ladder. The alternative was to walk up the ladder with it.

This was unsafe because of the way the old external pipes worked. Once you got it to the tip and secured it, you had to stretch and connect two sections of two-and-one-half-inch fire hose to supply water to it. These two sections of hose then had to be connected to a Siamese appliance that controlled the flow of water. Then another section of hose was connected to the Siamese appliance with a water supply.

It wasn't until all these tasks were complete that you could put the outriggers out and raise the aerial ladder out of the bed of the ladder truck. Then someone had to operate the ladder pipe itself by pulling on ropes to move the ladder pipe and direct the water stream back and forth and up and down. This appliance at the tip became an elevated water supply if needed.

There were many steps to this process. Generally, a whole crew would ensure it was complete before moving to another task. If you were putting up a ladder pipe, it was because the fire was large or the potential was there for the fire to progress in size. Little else could be accomplished on these large types of fires. When you used the ladder pipe, the fire was defensive and was fought outside the building. Whole crews would generally help in the procedure because no interior firefighting could be accomplished.

My first exposure to driving a fire truck came as a surprise. I was told to drive after only being on the job a few months. The program manager came by to do a surprise inspection of our station that day. The inspection included driving and pumping the truck, which I had never done before. Because the grade reflected our whole shift, I received a verbal lesson right before the evaluation. Prior to the verbal direction, I didn't even know how to start the truck.

I rarely backed down from a challenge. I wanted to do well so the members of my crew would accept me. Not knowing beforehand how to start the truck or pump one, I proceeded through the described steps.

I started the truck by turning on the batteries and simultaneously pushing the start button. Carefully I pulled out the truck always looking in the mirrors. I had to find the exact location on the street to line up with the door to back up, so I used a landmark to guide me.

I followed directions and backed the truck safely back into the bay. We passed the benchmarks to pass the inspection, and I earned some extra credit because the program manager stared at my breasts during the whole evolution.

The original intent was to see if I would back down and decline to drive. Perhaps the truck would have never left the bay and went on a call, but after the inspection, the captain left me in that position.

My size-up based on the experiences at the fire station was not to back down from any challenge presented to me. It was not always the safest decision to accept these challenges. I perceived it as a personal evaluation of my mental toughness, and if I didn't accept the challenge, I failed the test.

The tests threatened my continued employment and success with the fire service. I still had to meet the benchmarks of progress and competency to fulfill the requirements to come off probation. If these assessments weren't successfully completed, I could still be terminated.

I had no experience driving a fire truck in an emergency response mode, but I did it anyway. My perception of the speed the truck should operate on an emergency call was based on how it was normally driven. The very first call dispatched resulted in a quick response. That was the standard I had observed.

My perception of how to drive a fire truck was based on how others drove. Their example was the only training received. I drove as fast as my estimation the truck normally responded to calls. The captain looked surprised. He knew there had been no prior training. He shouldn't have put me in that position. I had only learned to drive a fire truck that day. My experience riding up front as the officer in charge was similar and completed within my first year in operations.

My captain rarely gave me any direction. My job was to get the hose line to the front door, get dressed, search for victims along the way, locate the fire, and make a fire attack. I learned this in recruit school. He would routinely look away and not answer if I asked him a question. He left me to figure out what to do next. He probably did it intentionally so that I would perform poorly and he could document it to eliminate me, but I thrived on the challenge and, fortunately, quickly progressed since I was confronted with making decisions early.

He only gave direction if I was doing something contrary to his will. Then he clearly let me know it! I had to make decisions on my own and do so quickly. His lack of guidance improved my capacity to problem solve.

He smoked a pipe the whole way to emergency incidents. He rarely put his breathing apparatus on. He wasn't a fan of wearing it. It was a tradition that was hard for him to break. I rarely saw him wear it, and when he did, he complained he had to stop smoking his pipe.

He would come inside to do a quick assessment of the fire without any breathing apparatus and then leave me alone to extinguish the fire myself. His lack of support left me to learn fire tactics myself.

He wasn't a good example of the importance of wearing personal protective gear (PPE). His philosophy was that breathing apparatus wasn't necessary, and if you wore it, you weren't a real firefighter. My firsthand experience taught me that your life might depend on it. Even with his efforts to persuade me otherwise, I wasn't influenced to stop wearing it.

Later this tradition would result in many firefighters developing some form of cancer. In the early days of firefighting, breathing apparatus wasn't available, but when it became available, many chose not to wear it.

Another practice was to leave the top clip of your coat undone and not wear your flash hood. The idea was to use your neck, ears, and face to feel how hot the fire was becoming. The skin of these areas was your thermostat. Firefighter PPE became so good it protected firefighters from extreme heat, masking the actual temperature in a structure. My captain kept his coat open so he could feel when it was getting too hot. He didn't wear a hood so that when his ears blistered, he knew it was getting too hot.

It was the traditional method to gauge fire conditions. His experience had taught him that was how to judge heat. Like him, a lot of the older firefighters couldn't break these early traditions. They didn't like the new PPE and didn't adopt the practice of wearing breathing apparatus or their protective gear.

His poor example of not wearing PPE didn't influence me, however, because of my personal experience in my recruit academy. My instructors had taught me an unintended valuable lesson. These observations about the reluctance to change traditions known to improve firefighter safety prepared me to receive new advances in the fire service when they came along.

One time, my captain arrived on the scene of a gas explosion with his whole coat open, smoking his pipe. The gas explosion had blown an entire wall off a large house. He complained he had to button up his coat and stop smoking his pipe.

I think because I worked hard and never gave up, my captain started to warm up to me. He gave me the direction to pull a larger hose line for this call, which was rarely used but should have been used more. There were many fires where larger hose lines would have been more effective. Big fires equal bigger volume of water provided in larger hose lines. You can't deliver the water volume to extinguish large fires with smaller hose lines. Large-diameter hose was another newer practice.

Knowing how my captain managed taught me not to question his decisions for me to drive and ride up front. He gave little direction, and the result was on-the-job training that gave me experiences to rapidly progress my intelligence about firefighting strategy.

When I first rode in the cab as the supervisor, most of the crew on the truck had been in the fire service longer than I'd been alive. I had a general idea which radio channel to be on and what benchmarks were communicated on the radio.

There were no computers on the trucks then. It was the captain's job to run the siren with a foot pedal. Some drivers prefer to do it, but it's a distraction from driving.

I gave updates to the dispatcher verbally. The breathing apparatus was mounted in the cab. They weren't mounted in the seat like in the rear jump seats. You had to turn and twist to get in and out of them. You could easily get tangled in the bracket with the straps of the breathing apparatus.

Once I overcame those logistics, I had to give directions, assignments, and commands to the crew. I communicated status reports and requests for additional resources on the radio. You had to establish command and run the incident until the chief arrived.

My knowledge was limited. Before this, my responsibilities had been limited to tasks like pulling the hose off the truck to the front door, getting dressed, and getting ready to go inside. Then there was a search for victims on my way to locate the fire. The door might have to be forced open, but that was generally assigned to the ladder crew.

I was now in charge of planning a strategy and assigning tactics. The first step was a size-up of the emergency scene. Then you had to make quick decisions on where to focus efforts and resources to support the strategy. The choice of tactics to support the strategy of victim location and fire control task assignments was given. Fires make themselves all too obvious, so like a moth to a flame, everyone would go.

I became pregnant on my one-year anniversary in the department as I came off probation. As directed by policy, I reported my condition to my captain. I was unsure of what my status would become. I was worried that I could still be dismissed since it was so close to just being taken off probation. I wasn't even sure if I could still be employed while pregnant.

I was afraid to report my condition, but also afraid not to. I had worked hard to fit in as one of the guys. My advancing pregnancy would make it more apparent I didn't fit into the traditional visual stereotype of a firefighter. I was afraid of the effects the smoke inhaled and absorbed would have on my unborn child as well. Just the shift before, we'd had three house fires in the same shift. One of the fires was extensive and required three bottle changes before the fire was extinguished.

I was afraid and anxious that I would be fired due to my condition. I was still afraid of losing my job. I had already sacrificed and put so much effort into keeping my job and succeeding. Because of the investment and cost paid, I was starting to develop a strong love for the fire service.

My captain called the chief and told him one of his firemen was pregnant. The chief was confused. He thought someone had called accusing one of the firemen of getting them pregnant.

The department only extended limited-duty assignments to injured firefighters. They weren't prepared to manage issues relating to women now being in the fire service. Fortunately, I was offered an administrative position, which I was grateful for. The fire chief was proactive in attaining and trying to retain the few women and minorities that existed in the department so it wouldn't have to be legally enforced. But just because he embraced diversity didn't mean the rest of the fire department did.

There were no maternity uniforms. Another female in the department who knew how to sew took one of my collared dress shirts and turned it into a maternity shirt. I purchased a pair of navy-blue maternity dress pants at a department store. That became the first department maternity uniform.

The driver pump operator school was coming up for my recruit class. This was a required class for all firefighters to attend and pass successfully to train you to drive and operate fire trucks. Classroom time was spent learning and practicing hydraulics. I had experience driving and pumping a fire engine, but I had not been taught hydraulics. I memorized the appropriate water pressures for each line without conducting any calculations. It was a good use of my time while on a limited-duty assignment. There was some practical application that required you to wear your turnout gear. The flap on the pants was unable to be secured due to the girth of my growing stomach.

During my limited-duty assignment, I organized and kept track of available fire units for the district chief during large fires. This occurred because of my own initiative and most resembled my actual job. The rest of the time I answered phones and general questions about the department. I spent time filing, reviewing, and rewriting some of the many policies that the fire department had. I became very familiar with the department policies through this process.

No one except the female civilian administrative staff ever mentioned my pregnancy. They were nice about it and held a baby shower in the office for me. I continued to stay productive and came up with some of my own projects because the department wasn't prepared for the situation. I was fortunate to actually get a limited-duty assignment since there are still some fire departments that don't offer limited-duty assignments to pregnant firefighters. I knew I was capable and wanted to do more.

Since I hadn't been in the fire department very long when I became pregnant, I had only accrued enough time to be paid for five weeks' maternity leave. I returned to work on the fire truck five weeks after I had my daughter. The size-up of my current situation identified my marriage wasn't doing well, and there was now a daughter I was responsible for. This became a driving force to work hard and secure my position.

After my limited-duty assignment when I returned to the station, I responded to many high-rise fire alarms that summer. Both sections of high-rise hose—at approximately thirty pounds apiece, the high-rise bag, and a set of irons had to be carried up one as many as fifteen stories of stairs several times a night during the shift. I would come back, and my hips would ache so bad I couldn't sleep.

I kept reminding myself that I needed to stay employed. It was becoming increasingly obvious that my marriage wouldn't last. I knew all too well I would be the only support for myself and daughter. I was determined to push through the pain and endure. I rationalized that certainly the effects of having a child would subside and I could eventually return to my normal level of productivity.

My husband and I continued to have financial and marital problems. My efforts were futile, working hard to support us. Even after the birth of my daughter, my husband continued the life of a single man. His car was at the after-hours clubs when the truck would go out in the middle of the night on calls. This weighed on my heart and mind. He was unfaithful and untruthful.

I eventually became tired of his behavior while I was working so hard to support us. The marriage ended, and I continued to be the sole financial support for my daughter and myself. The pressure to support us motivated me. It became more important than ever that I keep my job at the fire department.

The monetary benefit of working made all the difference in how I approached the physical and emotional challenges I encountered in the fire service, changing the amount of effort put forth to excel at work. The benefit of employment as a single mother outweighed the risks of navigating through an unwelcome environment.

CHAPTER SIX

Risk-Benefit Analysis

Before determining and initiating any fire-attack strategy, firefighters conduct a risk-benefit analysis. This is how they evaluate if what they are saving is worth the risk. Firefighters risk a lot to save a life. They do not take the same risks to just save property.

First arriving units do an evaluation of a structure to determine the likelihood of someone being trapped inside; things like the type of building construction and time the fire has been burning are considered to determine if the risk of sending firefighters inside is worth achievable results of finding and rescuing trapped occupants.

Sometimes if it is just a structure, although still monetarily a loss, it is not worth the risk of hurting or killing firefighters. When you do take the risks to conduct searches and rescues, consideration is given to the most severely threatened, the largest number of people affected, and those closest to the fire and in the most danger. That is how the priority of rescue efforts is decided.

The fire academy was tough and grueling because of the challenges I was presented with during the school. The instructors pushed you to do your best or resign. Resignation was not an option as I became the sole source of financial support for my family. I found my perception of what I thought the role of a firefighter was didn't line up with the reality of what I learned after I became one.

The battalion chief of training did a morning uniform inspection of new recruits. Each morning he would get really close to each recruit and closely inspect his or her uniform and hair for compliance with department policy. I had shaved the side of my hair to meet the specific requirements listed in the policy of my hair not touching the top of my ear. Each day he would blow in my ear when checking my hair for compliance with policy. I was surprised the first time it happened, and I was still trying to hold on to what I thought the moral character of a firefighter should be.

I thought perhaps I had imagined it the first time it happened. I came to realize it was exactly his intent. He later invited me to go to the National Fire Academy with him. At first, I was excited, thinking how fortunate I was to get to go to the fire academy so early in my career. I came to realize that since the fire academy was in a remote area, I was only invited to keep him company. I was disappointed in his behavior but also apprehensive about how to handle it.

I came up with a reasonable excuse for why I couldn't attend the fire academy with him. It was during my recruit academy. I told him I didn't feel I could miss time away from that but thanked him for the offer. He went on to ask another female firefighter to attend with him.

After my recruit fire academy, I didn't have any more incidents with him. He would go on to move out of the area and become a fire chief in another state. I realized I needed a strategy or plan of how to manage my fire career.

From the very beginning, I knew I needed a strategic plan to navigate through my fire service career. I had to decide when proposed with the question of whether I wanted to go to the fire academy as a guest and not as a participant what reputation I wanted to have within the fire department. I wanted to be taken seriously, and I employed the tactics of hard work and performed the tasks necessary to be considered a member of the department. My strategy was to excel at the tasks necessary to become a good firefighter and not become a fulfillment of some sort of quota of females in the fire service.

My parents taught me that if I was going to do something, I should do it right. To do anything less than my best would be a waste of time. Risk-benefit analysis helped me evaluate if what I was trying to attain was worth the price or risk to attain it. This assessment helps determine whether the end goal is truly desired and will bring happiness.

I had to decide in recruit school if the risk to my personal safety was worth the benefit of a career in the fire service. I evaluated the value of a productive, successful career versus just filling the status quo. I knew I could have some control over how my career went based on what decisions I made early on.

It was inappropriate to go with the training chief to the fire academy. I still had to be careful how I declined the offer to ensure my employment wasn't in jeopardy. I recognized during the recruit academy that policies were not always valued or enforced in the department. The lack of compliance to policy I witnessed by the training staff confirmed my belief.

Early in my career, I decided to make opportunities out of less desirable tasks. You can do the same type of risk-benefit analysis before you make serious decisions in your life. Decide if what you are trying to accomplish is worth the cost to achieve it. Only risk a lot when you are receiving a lot. The sacrifices should be worth the cost to achieve the desired goal.

Any firefighter who works over five years at the same fire station is considered eligible for a transfer during the annual transfer process. I found it difficult to consider volunteering for a transfer, especially since I had worked so hard to fit in at my present assignment. Even though my station assignment was at a desired location, I submitted a transfer because I wanted input on where my next assignment would be. The fire department conducted transfers every time there was a new recruit class or when there was a department need. This could occur annually.

I had joined a satellite group to support a newly formed technical-rescue team program that had been organized to have one designated station for all members to operate from and respond to calls. Team training and equipment maintenance would be performed at this station.

The fire chief wanted our department to be a part of a national movement to form more Federal Emergency Management Agency (FEMA) Urban Search & Rescue teams. At the time there were only two in the nation. Our department applied and became one of these new teams.

Firefighters involved on the team were told by the task force leaders on the team that if they were truly dedicated, they should seek a transfer to this new division and station. I would need to transfer from my current assignment. I submitted my transfer because I was dedicated to this new program and because I thought I could make a difference. This new assignment would be a challenge. Finding people overcome by smoke during a fire with no visibility was already challenging. Locating victims in a collapsed structure without special equipment would be even harder. This urban search-and-rescue team would acquire and train on new equipment that wasn't available on fire trucks to make search-and-rescue easier and more effective when there was a structural collapse.

Firefighters in my station believed they were the best in the department. Most firefighters in the department didn't understand or have the vision of technical rescue yet because special operations was a new concept that was still considered risky for firefighters, and the rescue techniques and methods weren't perfected, tested, or widely used yet.

When firefighters have pride in their individual capabilities and skills and their station as a whole, they become more competitive and improve their performance.

Because they were known to have their own personal agendas, some of the first people who introduced the concept of technical rescue weren't taken seriously by a majority of the department. Since technical rescue wasn't fully understood yet, firefighters in the department saw it as just another silly notion by these individuals to create a niche for themselves, the loftiness of their aspirations making it appear like an unattainable goal.

The purpose of the technical-search component was to detect and locate trapped victims so they could be rescued. No rescue breaking and breaching could occur until victims were located. The few females on the FEMA team were in this technical-search component as technical-search specialists, canine handlers, or in the medical component. My place on the FEMA team was secured by taking one of these positions. This position was seen as less desirable, but I was accustomed to accepting undesirable positions.

I became convinced of the benefit of an urban search-and-rescue team by my research of the technical-rescue equipment. At a product demonstration at the fire training center, a German man sold the only listening devices available and used on the teams at the time, personally showing the features and capabilities of the equipment and providing personal training with the equipment. He shared his story with me of how he became involved with the research to develop them because of his personal experience growing up in Germany.

He and his family had been trapped in their home for three days before anyone had known they were there and still alive after a bomb had exploded nearby and collapsed their house. His father had told them to all find a rock and to bang this rock on a structural member of the house until someone heard them. He'd noticed that when he banged on a metal pipe, the noise had been louder than on wood or concrete. This tactic had been what made it possible for others to locate and rescue them.

That is how he got the idea to use sound to locate lost and trapped victims in building collapses. He studied sound frequencies with help from others in the field. He helped engineer listening devices and was personally convicted of their usefulness and their ability to make a difference. He also convinced me of their usefulness. No amount of joking later could deter my commitment to encouraging the team to utilize this equipment in the search component. The personal story he shared convinced me of its effectiveness.

A fire captain in California developed the first search cameras. He used another one of the five senses to locate missing victims in structural collapses. His motivation was to get a visual confirmation that someone was trapped before the resources were committed to an extensive and lengthy rescue operation. The strategy was logical and practical, so it appealed to me. It was easy for me to identify its value and see its practical use.

The time I worked in support of the early technical-rescue team qualified me to be on this new team. It didn't occur to me then, but it was a risky move to also be one of the most junior members of the team. My confidence came from my success overcoming obstacles at my first assignment and the conviction I held about the effectiveness and need for a technical-search component to help ensure a trapped victim's detection and survival.

The team's success was made possible because a few members with vision were willing to transfer out of their current assignments and comfort zones. This commitment made the technical-rescue team a success. The program is still operational today, and I'm glad to have been part of its inception. The team not only includes a department component but also participates as a regional and FEMA team.

My old fire station was eventually torn down and replaced by a new building. A lot of people who were eventually promoted had made the decision to transfer and commit to the FEMA team. Many of the ones who stayed at my old station were not promoted, and the era of big fires ended with the old station and better fire protection systems. The ones who stayed represented the old, traditional values of the fire service that were so ingrained they were hard to change.

New technical-rescue team members were responsible for knowing all aspects of technical rescue, but many also branched out to learn special skills and knowledge that were key components of the FEMA team. Some of these included rope-rescue training, vehicle extrication, confined-space-and-trench rescue. The FEMA team specialized skill I chose was in the technical-search component.

This component worked with urban search-and-rescue canines, listening devices, and cameras. Few others wanted to fill that position. It didn't involve operating heavy equipment. The work was more intricate and involved more mental challenges than the physical challenges of the rescue component, which appealed to the testosterone levels of its members. A majority of the FEMA task force members were basic rescue component workers. That consisted of using heavy breaking-and-breaching equipment to access victims under heavy concrete and steel.

My size-up of the position identified it as essential. There wouldn't be competition to secure the spot. This reinforced my theory that taking less desirable positions can provide future opportunities.

Members of the rescue component gave me and the technical-rescue component little respect. The rescue component was considered the most important by members of that component. That was significant because the majority of FEMA team members were in the rescue component. There are several other FEMA team components for the whole team to operate efficiently. There is command staff, medical, hazmat, plans, logistics, communications, structural specialists, and the technical-search component.

Being involved from the very beginning allowed me the opportunity to research and make selections for purchasing the listening devices and cameras for the team. I became the most knowledgeable about the technical-search component.

As the only female assigned to the technical-rescue station, and not assigned to the rescue component on the FEMA team, the high-profile positions on calls were given to a select group of males who represented the team. This was the case even though I still held the same certifications and had completed the training required for the rescue component for my position on the technical-rescue team as a member of the station.

The consequence of not being in the rescue component on the FEMA team was that my function at the station was to support operations on actual calls. The same individuals rappelled down to make rescues on calls or rode in the back of the helicopter used for special rescue insertions even though I was trained and could perform the task. They were the ones who operated the cutting and spreading tools to gain access to patients during actual vehicle extrications.

I was accustomed to receiving the less desirable tasks on a team, but I used those experiences to gain knowledge that I was able to capitalize on later.

Other firefighters made derogatory comments about my worth to the team, and my supervisors further limited my opportunities to perform the key roles on calls. I chose not to respond to the negative comments. My reaction was controlled, so the message didn't deliver its intended response, and my apparent immunity to their attempts only made them mad. Maintaining control of my response put me at an advantage during the encounters. They became enraged, because no matter what they said, they couldn't get a reaction out of me.

Firefighters who worked with me became frustrated when they realized I didn't care what they thought. The intended damage to my confidence didn't weaken my resolve to continue my participation on the team. The tactic wasn't effective. My strategy became a focused effort to excel in my field, and membership on the team was one of the tasks required. Their cruel tactics didn't support my strategy. My tactical response was to not let someone else's opinion keep me from reaching my goal.

My experiences taught me to use the tactic of indifference to protect myself. My strategy was to achieve professional success. Being accepted as a member of the department was part of my strategy. Working hard, and overlooking injustices were tactics to achieve this goal. Having to protect myself was necessary while my strategy was being performed. Working in a hostile environment was just part of the expected price to pay. Fires are dangerous, but some of the daily tasks in the station were just as dangerous.

My strategy to overlook injustices started to produce results. Other firefighters' open hostility toward me warmed into tolerance or a realization I wasn't going away. I continued to excel in performing my job. This process was not without tactical errors or risks. My strategy required frequent size-ups to evaluate the tactical progress toward reaching the strategic goals. The tasks had to be performed in a dangerous environment, and there was a threat to my personal safety. Sometimes protecting exposures was the safest and only viable tactic available to manage the situation.

If outside exposures and fire extension could be controlled, the fire would be contained. If I could survive the attempts to break my resolve to remain a member of the team, I had a chance to change the perceptions of my worth on the team.

This tactic provided me with an additional measure of control. My presence became more upsetting to them than the effect of their efforts influenced me.

By design, women just aren't as strong as men. There are exceptions to every rule, but I found this to be true in my case. The challenges I accepted were emotional or intellectual not tests of strength. I excelled in intellectual competitions but knew my limitations in regards to physical strength.

I competed and excelled in the skills within my strength range. Technique, finesse, and agility were factors that put me at an advantage performing some tasks. I recognized this, and I was selective about the challenges that I competed in. Utilizing and rigging rope advantage systems was a better use of my skills than trying to lift heavy objects. My smaller size was an advantage in making entry into confined spaces, which was better than trying to operate the heavy tools required to break and breach concrete to gain access to a confined space.

The team would sometimes conduct special demonstrations for the public. The same few people generally performed these high-profile evolutions. That didn't stop me from continuing to participate as a team player.

I participated at one of these demonstrations where a high line was rigged and run off an elevated point to the ground. One of my teammates was riding the rope line down to the ground. He was having a hard time releasing the harness carabineer that connected him to the rope system he was riding down to the ground. I was pushing down on the high-line rope to relieve the tension so he could disconnect his carabineer and be free from the line.

Other personnel assisting in the operation had abandoned the line, but I continued holding down providing the release of rope tension to assist him. With my help, he was able to release his carabineer and get off the line. Once he was free from the rope, he suddenly let go of it, and a carabineer on the rope hit me in the face, and the carabineer opened and clamped on my nose.

The steel carabineer hit me so hard that my face was numb, and I couldn't feel it. The tensioned rope line was now somehow attached to my face. I had to reach up and follow the line to find where it was attached to my face so I could free it. This required that tension be held down on the line because the carabineer was still attached to my face. I found the carabineer attached to my nose but wasn't sure if it had punctured the skin and gone through my nose. The locking mechanism on the carabineer had actually gone up my nostril. I was able to disconnect it from my nose, but my nose immediately started bleeding.

A rappelling demonstration out of the helicopter was scheduled immediately after this high-line evolution. The rotation allowed for my participation. I was still bleeding, so I had to pass up the rare opportunity to participate in the rappelling demonstration out of the helicopter. It was more important that the crowd not see someone was hurt. The demonstration was supposed to show the capabilities of our team. The realities of what it took to be on the team were not as apparent.

The accident was never reported. The team leaders didn't want to report injuries because they were afraid of losing the technical-rescue program. Members of the team didn't want to risk the ability of the team to continue training, including myself. There were still some chief officers who were critics of the new program.

The training is how the team identified techniques to perform special operations and perfect our theories. We accepted the risk of accidents and injuries incurred by team members. The training was necessary to identify the best technical-rescue techniques. Getting injured was just part of the process, a sacrifice I was willing to take to be accepted on the team.

Not reporting injuries was an unspoken requirement to stay on the team. Personal safety wasn't made the first priority when conducting technical-rescue evolutions. Accidents weren't reviewed to ensure the same mistakes wouldn't be repeated because there was no record they occurred. There was no PIA of technical-rescue operations. This only reinforced the lesson learned in recruit school, which was that accident and PIA reports weren't utilized or used to improve operations or as designed to be used by our department.

A higher priority was given to end results, and I complied with the request for the sake of team integrity. There was still hope I could gain team acceptance by my loyalty. I would realize later that my strategy had not produced the hoped-for team acceptance by my peers.

My loyalty wasn't recognized. Many of the key players on the early FEMA team were later promoted with no other accomplishment than their membership on that team. I had been loyal from the beginning and had added value to other disciplines within the department. I had received higher certifications and education, but my efforts weren't rewarded the same way.

I needed to change my strategy. I showed my dedication by deploying on all FEMA activations, attending every training event, and keeping accidents secret, but my efforts were not rewarded. My dedication to the team ran as deep as anyone else's. I kept the secrets of the team.

Our team was one of the first FEMA teams formed, and it had a reputation for being one of the best. Our team was seen as experts by the other FEMA teams and within the technical-rescue community, yet most of the expertise came from a result of trial and error.

It wasn't really because the members of the team had exceptional knowledge. They did what was necessary to figure out a solution to the problem. As drills were conducted to perfect a skill, other questions came up, which led to more hands-on experiments that didn't always go well.

If anyone knew some of the dangerous things the team attempted, the team wouldn't have been as revered or allowed to continue. One of the team members wrote an entire book about rope rescue and hadn't proven, tested, or even tried the information presented in the book. There weren't any other books about rope rescue at the time, so there wasn't anyone else to challenge the concepts.

One particularly dangerous event involved a high line that wasn't tested first and included a team member being dropped off a ten-story building. There wasn't enough tension on the rope, and he hit the ground fast and bounced about twenty feet through the air before landing in the asphalt parking lot, where he was knocked unconscious. The helmet he was wearing saved him from further injury.

The first step before putting anyone on a high line is to load test it before anyone rode it. Luckily he wasn't killed. The same individual who wrote the book was involved in rigging the high line for this evolution.

In another incident, the bumper of a truck was used as an anchor. The two-thousand-pound-test-rated carabineer that was attached to the bumper of the truck was straightened, and the bumper was pulled away from the utility truck. The carabineer broke in half, and a large part flew across the bay.

Fortunately, it didn't hit anyone, only putting a dent in another one of the utility vehicles parked there. No one ever explained how the dent got there. The unauthorized attempts to fix the dent only made the dent worse.

These incidents were never documented, so there was false confidence that no one on the team would ever get in trouble. This exaggerated confidence from the experience of never getting in trouble seemed to influence supervisors' and participants' judgments while conducting some evolutions. This attitude was demonstrated by the dangerous operations engaged in by team members. There seemed to be few limits or parameters to keep our imagination within the bounds of what would be considered safe or reasonable when attempting a new skill.

Another incident occurred when the team practiced vehicle extrication behind the station. Each shift was given a junk vehicle with which to practice. The vehicles were prepped ahead of time by having all the fluids removed. During the training, all vehicles had their doors and roofs removed, and the dashes were pushed forward with vehicle extrication tools to allow more room to access the driver and passengers.

Once the training with the vehicle was complete, we used what was left of the vehicle to hone our skills on cutting the various types of car metal. The dash was pushed forward, so the car was left in the shape of an upside-down V. We accomplished this by making a cut in the baseboard of the vehicle, placed a spreading tool against a door post, and used the tool to push against the dash of the vehicle.

We frequently took the training farther than was necessary to accomplish the task.

Someone had an idea to put gas back in the cars and play bumper cars with them after there was little left of the vehicle, to create more vehicle damage. The hope was the damage would create a new challenge to access the driver and require additional vehicle extrication. The game of bumper cars continued until the car ran out of fuel, failed mechanically, or someone got hurt, and the drill evolved to include real patient care. The training was great but usually evolved past the point where training standards could be conducted safely.

The team was called to assist on many special assignments but wasn't designed to complete all the tasks requested that it perform.

A metal storage container at the training center had a partially collapsed roof that started leaking. The collapsed section of the roof provided a place for rainwater to collect. The weight of the water collecting there was pushing down that section of roof. The container resembled a cave with a rock slide inside. The interior looked like a dark and dirty mine. Pieces of rust dropped down on top of us while we worked, yet the rust is what held the roof in place.

The logistics division of the department stored equipment at the training center and wanted to use the container for excess storage. They requested that the technical-rescue team come and use one of our Airshores to push the roof back up in place. An Airshore is air-powered support jack that consists of two parts that slide past each other and adjust to the area they are used.

They work by using high-pressured air to push one side of the Airshore against a solid surface, and the other end slides to support an unstable surface. Airshores adjust to the size of the space they are used in. They can fall apart without a solid contact point and constant air pressure holding them securely in place.

These Airshores produce thousands of pounds of force per square inch. Normally you shoot an Airshore on a piece of placed wood timber to spread the force and pressure delivered by the Airshore, instead of all the force being delivered to just a small area.

Our team wasn't excited to perform the task. The job seemed beneath the capabilities of the team, so the job wasn't taken seriously, and our actions were complacent. No wood timbers were used between the Airshore and the contact point on the metal storage container.

My job was to shoot the Airshore. All that required was to depress a lever to allow air to enter the shore. I questioned not using any wood timbers but was ordered to shoot the shore. I followed the simple procedure to depress the lever to allow air to enter the shore when the order was given.

When the shore was shot, it punched right through the rusty metal roof and launched somewhere outside. The two pieces of the Airshore separated because there was no longer a contact point to stop it. Airshores strength comes from the firm contact that the shores provide under high air pressure against a stable surface.

The location of the launched Airshore couldn't be seen because our crew was inside the container working. There were three faces of disbelief inside that metal container. After what seemed like an eternity, the noise of that metal shore made a loud clanking sound when it hit the ground outside.

There was potential that the Airshore had hit something and caused serious damage or hurt someone. I felt responsible since I had been the one who'd pushed the button to activate the Airshore. This was reinforced by the other crew members who blamed me for the accident. I had activated the shore even though they gave the order and had placed the shore in its position without support or shoring.

Technicians are responsible for picking the location and placing the Airshores. They ensure the shore is in position and ready. They hold the two loose, unsupported ends of the shore together so they line up and don't malfunction. They decide on placement and the surface the shore is placed on. They give the order for the shore to be activated, but somehow it was still my fault.

Thankfully, the Airshore didn't hit anything else before it struck the ground. It felt like an eternity to confirm this because no one dared look outside for fear of being struck in the head by the Airshore falling from the sky. The container now had more damage than when we arrived. It had a big hole in the top, and there was nothing to stop the rainwater from coming in at all.

The standing rainwater had allowed the water to accumulate and caused the roof to rust, diminishing the strength of the metal. This rusty section couldn't support the force of the Airshore being shot directly on it. To remedy the problem, the crew covered the hole with a sheet of plywood. The importance of using wood timber to share the force delivered by an Airshore was reinforced that day. The type and placement of the wood used that day was just different than how it should have been used. This is one example of how the technical-rescue team gained their expertise about shooting Airshores.

One rappelling training evolution included testing a new communications system. It was tested while performing night-insertion operations. The evolution entailed rappelling out of a helicopter with a medical pack and then being picked back up after the patient was secured and packaged in a Stokes basket for transportation under the helicopter. The crew and patient rode out of the forest dangling from the end of a rope under the helicopter. The location of the patient was deep inside a heavily covered tree area. The branches of the tree were as large as trees trunks.

The accident happened because we were using a single-rotor police helicopter that wasn't designed for these kinds of operations. It was underrated for the weight that was put underneath it.

The helicopter was trying to pull us out of the trees, but we became entangled in the large branches. The branches were large enough to break our arms and legs if we hit them on our ascent. Our helmets were on, but there was still potential for sustaining a head injury because of the size of the branches and speed of our assent. We had no control of the speed we were lifted through the branches or where we were dragged through the trees.

We became entangled in the branches, which attached the helicopter to the trees. The pilot descended to allow us to untangle the rope from the branches. As soon as we were free from the dense branch tree cover, the helicopter tried to ascend with us through the dense cover.

The pilot struggled to hover because of the lack of air between the helicopter blades and the top of the trees. We received bumps and bruises but were finally clear of the trees. Because of the difficulty the pilot had hovering, the helicopter already had forward motion.

We swung out of control as the momentum of the helicopter yanked us free from the trees. The pilot was unable to compensate from the overexaggerated swinging caused by yanking us free. He had problems maneuvering, and the helicopter was essentially being pulled from the sky. The pilot had to land immediately or crash, and we were being taken with him.

We were on a backswing as the helicopter descended, which caused us to swing very quickly and slam into the ground. The helicopter couldn't hold altitude, so we were dropped faster and harder than we should have been.

The only light provided that night was fluorescent sticks. Members watching the training could see how fast we were moving by those fluorescent lights, and they feared our deaths or at least anticipated we would have serious injuries.

Fortunately, there were medical packs with rescue equipment on our backs that swung us around because they were heavy, and the packs made the first contact with the ground. Those packs took a lot of the impact and acted as shock absorbers when we slammed into the ground, preventing us from receiving serious if not fatal injuries.

The communication system we were testing was attached to a glove and worked by making a fist to push a button in the palm of your hand when you wanted to talk. I had been bracing up for a hard landing and had been holding the rope, so I was squeezing the push to talk on the radio.

I braced for a hard landing, squeezing the rope we were attached to tightly, trying to pull myself up and away from the ground. I was inadvertently squeezing the talk button on the radio system we were evaluating. I was very concerned, and it showed in my voice. My teammate was powerless to help as he listened to us yelling for the helicopter to pull back up. There were confusing rustling noises, thuds of impact, and grunts and groans mingled with my pleadings.

The helicopter blades were dangerously close to us when it landed. This evolution requires the spy line to be one hundred feet long, allowing the rescuer to be under the helicopter far enough to be clear of the blades but close enough to not hit objects hidden from view beneath it. The helicopter blades are very close to the ground especially near their end when the helicopter is on the ground.

We were dropped where the tips of the helicopter's rotor blades swing close to the ground. The helicopter had lost power and landed hard on the ground with the blades almost on top of us. Miraculously no one was seriously injured. The incident was never reported or talked about again. Loyalty to the team and its members prevailed over any of my safety concerns for my personal well-being.

The code to be a member of the team required loyalty and secrecy about close calls. Water operations were performed without any special equipment or training, and no known ability of the members to swim. Individuals were dropped in the middle of the ocean even during high seas. There was no prior training before this was attempted. Between the rotors blades pushing the water and high seas, members sometimes jumped and hit the bottom of a swell, and actually hit the bottom of the ocean.

I was left alone for long periods in the ocean with no communications and no flotation device. One incident involved two team members playing a dunking game to keep me under water when I was already tired of treading water.

Silly as it seems, I offered to be one of the last to be retrieved from the water after this water drill. Some were not as comfortable in the water, and there was an unspoken badge of toughness to be one of the last to be retrieved. I knew there would be a price to pay for demonstrating dominance, so I was not surprised by the dunking game that followed. If anything, I was getting mentally prepared and trying to save energy by treading water for what was sure to come.

On another evolution while on a spy line underneath the bottom of a helicopter, I was dropped really hard and dragged across concrete. I had already experienced a hard landing with the helicopter, so that was what I compared this landing with. It was not good judgment to conduct evolutions on concrete, but my prior experience gave me a gauge of how serious it was. I judged the incident to be less serious than my prior experience because I received fewer scrapes and bruises this time.

I found myself in a position to have to physically defend myself at the station one day, which only enforced the perceived need to become physically and emotionally tough. The incident was witnessed by others, but no one intervened on my behalf. Another firefighter almost broke my arm. He was mad because of something I'd said. My verbal defense was an effective weapon. This incident was never discussed past its occurrence, but I received a long-term injury from the encounter.

He twisted my arm abruptly and forcefully behind my back as one would do to handcuff someone, and held my arm in this uncomfortable position pushing my arm up toward my shoulder blades in an unnatural position.

Many of the first FEMA members joined the team at their own expense and bought their own equipment. They voluntarily went on deployments before the team's formation without compensation and used their own personal leave to respond to deployments.

A couple of individuals were particularly bad examples and weren't team players. They were visionary people, and while they accomplished a lot for the technical-rescue program, they were driven by their own motivations. They ultimately capitalized on the new field of technical rescue and started a company and became some of the leading experts in the field.

Their motivation had more to do with personal benefit than making discoveries and improvements in technical rescue that benefited lost and trapped individuals in structural collapse during catastrophic events. They needed the help of the other technical-rescue personnel involved at the time to attain their goals. The rest of us were more than happy at the time to advance the concept of technical rescue since it was a new field.

In the early days of the team, our first equipment was donated by local vendors. The gesture was self-serving because they hoped the favor would be repaid by the team making future equipment purchases with them. Later, normal purchasing procedures weren't followed so the favor could be repaid without going through the normal bid process.

Those who started their own company would take these early equipment donations given to start the team and use the equipment for their personal business. They held technical-rescue classes through their business and utilized on duty technical-rescue team members to teach the class. Any members off duty helped without receiving compensation because we craved the training.

The team members who owned the business and set up the class were getting paid by both an outside party and the city on the days they worked.

They were captains, so they directed the firefighters working for them to help teach the class.

The off-duty personnel were taking a large personal risk. If anyone had been injured while assisting with this training, it wouldn't have been considered an on-the-job injury. We would have incurred the financial cost of the medical bills as well as the loss of work. The nature of the training involved dangerous tasks that routinely presented the potential for injury.

Ultimately because members were tired of being taken advantage of, they refused to help them anymore. The team was missing some equipment to perform an actual rescue on an emergency incident. The equipment had been taken to use at a class the company was teaching. It was equipment that was donated by one of the vendors that was inventoried to the team. They had taken the equipment for self-serving reasons. They had lost the vision of the purpose of the team. This incident resulted in the refusal of team members to help them anymore.

The captains chose to place blame instead of apologizing. The officers responsible for the team that had committed the offense identified the problem with the team not getting along between the shifts as group dynamics instead of the real problem of their misuse of team equipment for personal use. They used city money designated to the team for members to attend a mandatory team-building class offered at one of the local psychiatric hospitals. The hospital itself was a secure facility with a barbed wire fence. No one on the team wanted to attend. One team-building class wasn't going to fix the kind of problems being experienced by the team.

Spending money on the class was money that could have been spent buying needed equipment. The exercises utilized by the facility weren't capable of fixing the problems the team was experiencing, because the facilitators didn't understand the real problems the team was facing. They were told the team had problems with team unity. They weren't given all the details of why the team integrity was broken.

During the class, plans were discussed of how a rope system could be built to escape the facility. No one on the team was interested in any team-building game unless it presented a challenge of some sort. The most humorous thing about the class was that at the end of every evolution there would be an evaluation time when each team member would have to describe his or her feelings about the evolution.

It was entertaining to me because it was apparent that members of the team had no idea of what the facilitators were talking about when they wanted us to express our personal feelings. Team members were passionate about the team, but personal emotions were not part of the criteria required during operations.

The parameters did not allow us to just use the word *good*. When someone figured out a word that was acceptable to the facilitators, the rest of the team would all use the same word. The whole thing was hilarious to me. No one but me appreciated the humor in the exercise.

The team might have benefited from team-building training. The team certainly needed help. Our group was failing as a team. Every task given on the day of this training was accomplished by cheating. To the team, nothing else mattered but winning. Because the tasks were outside the comfort zone and expertise of the team, the team improvised to win. Eventually, the evaluators grew tired of our lack of compliance and participation.

I participated in an impromptu game of basketball that was initiated during our lunch break. There was full-contact basketball accompanied by fistfights. This was after a whole morning of exercises to improve team dynamics. Fighting had become the team norm, and the desire to fight didn't change after the training.

The captains who set up the training claimed success at the completion of the training. The evaluators who watched us were visibly disgusted. The team's behavior placed us at the intelligence level of a lab rat. To the outside world, we appeared polished. My personal experience was much different, so why did I think it was so important to be accepted as a member of this team?

As the most knowledgeable and with the most experience with the technical-rescue component, I attended the first FEMA technical-search-specialist certification class and was asked to fill a position on the newly formed working group, which I held for five years. The group was responsible for determining the testing standards and minimum qualifications required for the urban search-and-rescue canines. Even with my knowledge and experience in the component, I was never deployed as the search-team manager.

Some of the newly transferred captains assigned at the station were new to the program, so they weren't trained in many of the components on the team, but they were still made component leaders due to their rank. My captain in the station became the search-team manager, so he required my help. He relied on my expertise so he could manage the component since he didn't possess any knowledge of how the component actually worked. The same arrangement continued when another captain transferred to the station. He was given the title but was only able to make decisions based on my direction.

This wasn't the case in all manager positions on the team. The rank structure on the FEMA team didn't always comply with the fire department rank structure. In other components, there were lower ranked individuals running as the manager of components. They were given the positions because they were well liked by the task force leaders.

It wasn't always what you knew but who you knew. Even after being promoted to captain, I was never deployed as the manager of the component, although still active on the team. It was something never attained, even though I was qualified for the position. Even committing to the team at its inception couldn't overcome the gender bias that existed on the team. Being a loyal team player couldn't break the traditions held tightly that prevented me from being considered a full member of the team.

In the size-up of my current status, I weighed the continued risk against the benefit of my membership on the team. My current strategy had not altered their attitude. After a complete evaluation, I knew I'd made all the strategic corrections possible. I'd willingly taken less desirable duties and was loyal to the team. My size-up revealed that the goal of becoming a search-team manager was not attainable and there was not a strategy or any tactics that would work. Outside influences outside of my control prevented my successfulness in changing the current mentality. There wasn't a sufficient water supply to put this fire out.

The integrity of the team continued to decline. Personal friendships and favors were extended to less knowledgeable members. Friends of the task force leaders were chosen for deployments even though they hadn't attended required training. The task force leaders were poor examples for team members.

On the way home from a deployment, the task force leaders drove a support vehicle and led a convoy of our team's trucks and equipment. They had a cooler full of beer and drank on the ride back. Other members of the team copied their behavior. They took some alcohol out of a hotel they had searched so they would have something to drink on the long bus ride home.

By the time the team stopped at the first rest area, most members were visibly and highly intoxicated. The team physician had given each team member a Valium so they could relax on the long ride back. The result was concerning. The mix of alcohol and prescription medication had a depressing effect on some team members.

Members of the team started competing to go on deployments just to be paid the overtime. This was not why the team was originally formed and not why I committed to joining the team. The team was formed to utilize attained knowledge and skills to locate and rescue trapped structural collapse victims.

I sized up that my efforts could be better utilized somewhere else, so I pursued my college education. This qualified me for promotion when others at the station were not. They were considered the favorites in technical rescue but not eligible for promotion. They were given the manager positions on the FEMA team instead.

I had given the technical rescue and FEMA team my best effort, but it wasn't enough. It was time to plan a new strategy. I finished my bachelor's degree, pursued a promotion, and was transferred.

I took a chance accepting a transfer to help form a new team. There was no guarantee of its success. I took chances in my professional life. Even after my promotion and subsequent transfer, I continued to work toward the team's success. This required dedication and long-term commitment. When things got hard in my personal relationships, I didn't just quit. I worked toward resolution.

Becoming a member of the FEMA team required me to be competitive, which paid off later and resulted in my promotion. I gained a reputation for being emotionally intelligent. I proved I could make decisions logically and not be influenced and driven by emotions.

I chose which battles to engage in and focused on the ones there was a chance of winning. The ones chosen were the ones I could most influence and had identified as most beneficial.

My resolve to be a team player resulted in holding a position on the technical-rescue team for over eight years and for almost twenty years on the FEMA team.

Competition drives people to do unpredictable things. Don't underestimate the efforts of others to fight for the nozzle so they can put the fire out. Some competition is good and drives people to do their best, but don't underestimate the efforts of others to get ahead. If safety is sacrificed, it is too high of a price to gain admittance to a team.

My experience of shooting the Airshore through the metal container reinforced that safety practices should be followed. This event improved my knowledge of what had already been learned through my experience in recruit school.

It takes courage to act. Peer pressure to conform was a driving force in my decision making. The incident with the helicopter should have been reported. The capability of the helicopter to perform rescue operations was eventually identified. The insurance company refused to insure the helicopter to conduct those types of evolutions. Thankfully, this was discovered before another accident occurred.

Firsthand experience can teach lessons to help you in future situations. My near-miss incident with the helicopter helped me evaluate future helicopter operations, just like my experience in recruit school helped me identify flashovers in future fires. The knowledge gained from these experiences can help you handle future emergencies that occur.

My integrity was challenged. Taking donated equipment was an abuse of city resources, just like not reporting accidents. If your goal is to belong to a group no matter the cost, it may require the sacrifice of your integrity. Preplan now what you will do when presented with difficult choices. Plan a strategy to achieve your goals without sacrificing personal integrity.

You can control how you react to a situation. Not everything will go according to the strategic plan. Sometimes assigned tasks aren't fair. Strategic plans aren't always successful and need to be reevaluated to correct tactics that aren't working. There is more than one way to attack a fire.

Conduct risk-benefit analysis to weigh the costs of the strategy. If what you sacrifice isn't worth the benefit received it isn't worth the risk. The risk hazard assessment will identify the benefits of conducting an interior attack. Sometimes you can only initiate a defensive attack.

Size up what the desired goal is. Identify the hazards before you start the fire attack. Others will try to diminish your accomplishments. Be ready to extend more effort than others to attain your goal.

Take hard assignments with people you don't even like or get along with. You can learn something from the experience of working with them. You may learn you don't want to be like them.

You have something to contribute to any team. There will be something only you can accomplish. If you can no longer add anything to the team, it may be time to switch teams.

The years spent on the technical-rescue and FEMA teams taught me about loyalty to a team. It proved that loyalty could be valued more than anything else. We strive for the values of loyalty, honor, and valor. Consider if what you are defending is worth your loyalty and the required cost of your personal integrity. If something you are defending is immoral or illegal, evaluate your participation in the activity.

I evaluated the experiences in my life and tried to learn something from each one of them. It helped me be better prepared for the next incident that occurred. There is something to be learned from every trial or hardship faced. It's like a refining fire. The refinement process includes continuous melting and compressing of metal so you can form it into something else. The end result can be beautiful.

CHAPTER SEVEN

Escape Plan

Early in my career, most of my initial strategies were defensive, but the fire was now being contained enough to engage in some offensive attacks.

While at the technical-rescue station, I took a positive, effective offensive approach and made time to continue my education. I completed a bachelor's degree in six years during my eight years at this busy station. Education was not a prerequisite to get promoted at the time, but it was something I pursued to ensure my marketability. Firefighting is a physically demanding job, and I wanted to be qualified for other employment if anything physically prevented me from continuing my employment in the fire service.

I was engaging in dangerous operations at the technical-rescue station and receiving some injuries. The injuries didn't require medical treatment, but they made me realize an injury could prevent me from continuing a career in the fire service. With a small child and no other monetary support other than my job with the fire department, I strategically planned to pursue my formal education to ensure life's necessities could be provided in the event I was no longer physically able to perform the job of a firefighter.

Most people during this time were pursuing their advanced-life-support (ALS) paramedic certification. At the time you had to volunteer two twelve-hour EMS shifts to be able to practice off the engine. EMS was a separate department, had the medical director, and handled the transport of patients.

I started taking one class at a time when my daughter was in preschool. I opted not to take an easier curriculum. I wanted to secure a good education from an accredited university that would be recognized in the workforce.

I had to do my school homework late at night because of the workload required at the technical-rescue station. Other stations didn't have this additional workload. The cache of equipment was kept at the station. The equipment maintained a regular maintenance and inventory schedule. The maintenance and proficiency in the use of the equipment added to the workload at the station. Later, when formal higher education became a requirement for promotion, the extra effort paid off, and I was one of the few eligible people for promotion.

In spite of my perceived worth at the station, I was promoted to captain. Others who hadn't planned had to play catch-up to become eligible for promotion. Several opted for quick online educations from institutions that didn't have accreditation. It was all the fire department required at the time.

There was a lot of dialog that I only got promoted because I was a female. No consideration was given that my education, time in service, or special team experience had qualified me for the position. Whatever the reason, I tried to exceed the expectations of the position.

The truth was the male firefighters saying this hadn't met the qualifications to participate in the promotion process. They hadn't pursued a formal education or participated in any specialty teams or programs in the department. I was transferred to another station after my promotion and ran many calls. A lot of experience was gained because of managing personnel. Personnel issues became more challenging than running fire calls.

Shortly after becoming promoted to captain, I remarried. My new husband was another captain in the fire department. Apparently, someone had noticed my efforts and was impressed by them.

My first assignment as a captain was at the city's administrative buildings complex. Many of the people there had more seniority. My first test by the crew happened in the back of the fire station. They were outside on the back ramp smoking cigars.

New members of the fire department were required to sign an agreement not to smoke or chew tobacco products. There were some firefighters who were exempt from the requirement because they had been hired before the requirement, so they could still use tobacco products. Spittoons filled with spittle from tobacco chewing could frequently be found in the station. Chewing tobacco was a tradition some firefighters still engaged in. They would leave chew in their cheek while they fought fire even with their face piece on.

This was significant because one of the firefighters smoking with them had signed a no-smoking waiver. The purpose of the smoking waiver is to fulfill the requirements of the heart-and-lung bill that medically and financially covers firefighters if they get cancer or have a heart attack. Smoking is a risk factor for both. So not smoking helps prove that a diagnosis of cancer or heart disease wasn't caused by personal use of nicotine products.

Cancer is a real possibility for firefighters due to the type of work they do. Smoke from ordinary household items becomes toxic when burning. The smoke can actually be absorbed through the skin, and can be cancer causing. To be covered by the insurance bill, the insurance company wants to ensure the cancer you get could only have been caused by something you came in contact with while fighting fires.

This firefighter who was smoking in spite of his agreement was on the current list to be promoted to captain. Another senior firefighter on the promotion list was also outside smoking. Their actions were disrespectful. It challenged me to take action.

I called the junior firefighter who was smoking into the office and extended the courtesy of a verbal warning. I told him that if he was caught smoking again, he would be disciplined and no longer eligible for promotion. His smoking could be a cause for dismissal.

The senior member had been in the department long enough to be able to smoke. I still had a conversation with him about appearances. The appearance of smoking cigars outside the fire station didn't fit the professional conduct required of an officer. I reminded him to be a better example to younger impressionable firefighters.

Due to the way I handled the incident, our relationship became one of mutual respect. I often asked his opinion or advice in front of the whole crew and frequently took the advice.

The battalion officer's living quarters were in this station. The battalion chief hadn't stopped the smoking and didn't address the issue. Personnel matters in the station were the captain's responsibility. It was my job as the captain to enforce the rules. The captain could be held accountable for not enforcing the policy.

Which policies the department enforced was confusing. The chiefs didn't consistently enforce the rules, but they held others accountable for not enforcing them. Some people were not required to follow policy, but that depended on who they were.

A short time later, a group of firefighters was smoking at a Christmas party. The deputy chief was smoking and drinking with them. By his participation, he condoned the behavior. He was not a good example of a leader. He didn't correct the behavior, so it sent mixed messages about the importance of the policy.

He lacked the leadership abilities to make hard decisions or enforce policy or rules. It made others question how important following policies were because they weren't enforced at the top.

There were times when a policy was challenged because senior chiefs would discipline a lower ranking officer for not enforcing the rules they didn't enforce themselves. Policies were not equally enforced across the department. Not all polices were enforced, so it made them appear unimportant. It became confusing about what policies were expected to be followed.

If the senior chiefs liked you, it didn't matter if you followed policies. If you weren't liked, you could commit a minor violation and be disciplined. There was no consistency in policies enforcement.

I sized up it was safest to follow policy. They were in place for a reason. It was hard to complain about that management style because the policies were being followed. It allowed for consistency, which resulted in fairness. Sometimes you have to do hard things because it is simply the right thing to do.

Some policies were changed to accommodate certain individuals. Chiefs lost the trust and respect of members when it occurred.

The usual flow at fires is to attempt aggressive, offensive interior attacks and then transition to defensive exterior operations if progress can't be made and crews are losing the firefight. Most of my early years were defensive in nature due to the constant efforts to get me to fail and leave the fire service. With knowledge and experience, I was able to plan offensive attacks that were more effective.

During my first year as a captain at my first assignment, a call came in for a fire at the address of the house my ex-husband and I used to own. It was a call for an odor of smoke. It was the middle of the night, and the odor had awakened the occupants. These types of cases can be tricky. All types of approaches to rule out fire causes have to be investigated.

Sometimes it is hard to determine what the cause of the odor is. All the operating systems of the house were working correctly. The heating, cooking, and panel box were checked. Nothing could be found. After about an hour, the only thing that could be determined was that a piece of clothing had started heating up on the top of a halogen lamp. The trucks went back to the station with the resolve that the lamp was the culprit.

I couldn't go back to sleep. The thought that our diagnosis was wrong occupied my thoughts. The potential that later another call for a house fire at the same address would be dispatched concerned me. It was troubling because no definite, specific cause could be found. I didn't think anyone would believe a cause couldn't be found. They would think it was negligent or suspicious because of the circumstances.

I was lying awake, tossing and turning, feeling that something wasn't right. I decided to get out of bed. At almost the same time, the bells went off for a call. I held my breath and waited, hoping it wasn't the same address. It wasn't my old address but a house fire with a report of people trapped.

The call was in a remote area. It was the dead of the night right before people get up for early work shifts, the eerie time when many fire fatalities occur. Time is suspended and freak things happen. It is a time when no one is awake for any reason.

The detail report from the dispatcher gave me confidence that what she was saying was true. The report described a well-involved house fire along a stretch of isolated beach quite a distance from us. We would still be the second units arriving. The first unit would be by themselves for about ten minutes, which can be an eternity.

The house was occupied, although not all houses were in the off-season. A mother and her teenage daughter were unaccounted for and thought to be still inside. Perhaps this was the feeling of dread that had prevented me from going back to sleep.

The station emptied the house and took the tanker. A tanker is a truck that holds more water than the standard fire-attack engine provides. It can set up a portable tank and shuttle water to the fire-attack engine. Our station bordered some areas that didn't have a city water supply. That is why the station had a tanker. This area had some hydrants, but all areas weren't covered.

There was not an actual house number given since someone was only driving by and had seen the flames. The block number was the only information provided. The tanker was dispatched since an actual house number couldn't be identified to verify the area had hydrants.

A roll call was completed on the tactical channel. Then everyone waited for the first unit to arrive on the scene. It was still a long way from their station. It was at the end of their response area. There was only one way in and one way out of the area, and then the road ended. You had to decide to either turn right or left. Most of their area was to the right of their station. This fire was to the far right of their area.

After what seemed like an eternity, the first fire unit confirmed the reports of a well-involved house fire with victims reported inside. They relayed a message to us that they had laid into the fire with their supply hose. They stopped and left the end of their supply hose and drove to the fire. Laying a supply hose in is the right thing to do when it is a confirmed fire and you can visibly see flames.

They were requesting that our unit complete the connection to the hydrant and turn it on so they would have a water supply. This cuts down on the amount of time they would have to wait to receive a sustainable water supply.

As the second truck arriving, it was anticipated that our task would be to make this connection. Since an actual address wasn't given, I was reading the map, trying to locate hydrants near the block number given. There were no computers with GPS tracking and routing yet.

When our truck made the right-hand turn, you could see flames leaping in the air even though the house was still several miles away. The houses in this area are on stilts to save the homes from tidal erosion caused by flooding in storms.

It was a surprise to see how far their hose was from the house on fire. Their five-inch hose was lying in the street, and the burning house was still at least another mile down the road.

The message given to us by the first arriving truck was to pick up their supply line and finish the connection to the hydrant. They had used all one thousand feet of supply hose they carried on their truck. They needed us to make up the difference between where their hose stopped and to complete the connection to the hydrant. Then a connection could be made between our truck and theirs.

If the distance had been less than one thousand feet to the fire, it was customary at the time to just connect the supply house directly to the truck. If the hose line was over one thousand feet, the policy was to pump through the line. If a residential fire was large with flames well involved, you generally pumped through your truck to the attack truck. This becomes a backup if the pump on the primary fire unit fails. This allowed the second truck to pump right through the first truck and not disrupt fire operations.

The attack truck had grossly misjudged the distance from where they left the end of their hose to the house on fire. They should have been able to see the large of amount of fire that was visible. Later, the driver said he thought that was the closest known hydrant to the house on fire, so he laid his hose from there.

The end of his thousand feet of supply hose was still a long way from the structure on fire. Hydrants were hard to find because sometimes they were hidden behind sand dunes. The wind would blow sand and cover the hydrants. The wind had contributed to the intensity and spread of the fire itself.

There were actually hydrants every five hundred feet in this area. There was a hydrant just two hundred feet behind the structure. My driver was making plans to connect to the end of their supply line and lay our thousand feet of hose as directed. I stopped him from following their request.

The end of their hose was still too far away. Even if our thousand feet of hose was used, it still wouldn't reach the fire. I could see from studying the map that there were hydrants every five hundred feet. I was trying to locate a hydrant closer to the fire when a report came from the attack engines driver that he couldn't find the rest of his crew.

He had tried to make radio contact with them. There was no response. Now there were missing firefighters. I changed my priority. I directed my driver to take me directly to the fire and then to lay out from the attack engine to the next nearest hydrant past the fire.

The tanker was with us. I directed them to temporarily supply the attack engine that was now out of water. The fire was aggressively free burning. There were twenty- and thirty-foot flames jumping from the roof, being driven by the wind. With the tanker giving the attack engine their twelve hundred gallons of water, it allowed time for our engine to locate the hydrant and start pumping and flowing to the attack engine.

As soon as the engine left their end of the hose at the fire scene, the driver of the attack engine connected it to his truck, so my driver knew he could charge the hose line without hesitation. In the meantime, the tanker driver made the connection to the attack truck and gave its water supply to it until a permanent water source could be secured.

When we arrived on scene, the attack engine was in the middle of the road instead of to the side as it usually is so other units can pass. It was hard for our driver to maneuver around them. Driving past gave me a three-sided view of the structure.

The driver had parked in the middle of the street because the flames were so intense he was afraid the heat would melt the paint off the side of their truck. As our crew walked back to the attack engine, one of their crew members was walking toward me. He had his PPE on but wasn't on air. He was talking excitedly, which was his nature. I asked him where the rest of his crew was. He responded he didn't know. Except for being excited, he appeared all right.

My crew was directed to find the lost firefighters and to put some water on the fire.

Everyone except the driver on the other truck was filling in that day. They didn't normally work at that station. Many fire fatality reports list crew's ability to work as a team as a contributing cause in firefighter line of duty deaths. Another one is poor communications. The attack crew was not answering the radio. There were already two risk factors that could result in a firefighter fatality present at this fire.

My goal was to locate the missing firefighters, contain the fire, and search for fire victims. The likelihood of survival for the occupants was dim. The occupancy was fully involved, and fire was spreading to nearby homes. The fire crew was still missing and couldn't be raised on the radio.

It was hard to put together what had occurred on the scene. There was an empty water can thrown in the yard. A water can was not something that would be used to put out this amount of fire. The hose line was burned in half. The driver was running around making the new water supply connections. A ladder was lying on its side abandoned. The crew couldn't be seen.

I walked around the rear of the structure to do a walk around and found the missing crew. They were exterior of the building but couldn't hear any radio communications due to the loud noise of the fire burning. The wood burning in the house was crackling and popping. Neighbors were yelling for us to help them keep the flames off their houses. The drop down of burning materials caused several brush fires.

About this time the battalion chief arrived on scene. My crew defensively attacked the outside of the structure with a large-diameter hose and knocked down a large amount of the fire. Then we used a smaller line to enter the structure from the rear, where the building was mostly intact. We had to use a ladder because the exterior stairs had burned away.

Crews completed an interior fire attack and made a search of the building. This was the earliest it could be completed due to the volume of fire. Some of the fire had to be extinguished first.

The scene had been out of control upon our arrival. The first responding crew had tried to make an interior fire attack, but they had quickly run out of water. The water can had been used to put out the fire hose that had caught on fire. The ladder had been used to access the building because the stairs leading to the door had already started to burn.

The firefighter walking down the street had received burns. He had tried to advance up the stairs to the house when the fire flashed. He had turned away and received burns to his back, arms, and neck. He didn't have a hood or face piece on. Because it had just happened, blisters hadn't formed yet. He wasn't even aware he'd received burns. The scene was out of control so his excitement level appeared normal for the situation.

Unfortunately, the mother and her teenage daughter perished in the fire. The mother had actually exited the structure but had gone back inside to look for her daughter. The daughter was found underneath the back bedroom window where our first fire streams were focused. The mother was found in the threshold of her bedroom. Nothing had gone well, and nothing could be done to save them. The fire was too well involved upon our arrival. The conditions of the home and the amount of fire visible were too large to sustain life.

A fire hydrant was later found two hundred feet behind the residence. The hydrant used was three hundred feet beyond the residence.

This residence was burning during the time I was restless and unable to go back to sleep. If we had been dispatched while leaving our prior call, our unit would have been closer, and we would have gotten there sooner. The time difference could have improved their chance of survival.

This fire hadn't been detected yet. There is a sculpture of a sea monster in the front yard of a house just down the street from where this fire occurred. A fire monster had taken the lives of two people. It was the only one who knew the house was burning, yet the sea monster just stared and watched.

My pattern of restlessness before fire calls continued even without the help of noisy relay systems.

The burned firefighter taxed the battalion chief (BC) when he arrived. The firefighter started feeling pain and realized he was burned. He recognized his gear was damaged, and he now had blisters forming. He didn't know what to do so he walked up to the BC for assistance.

There was no one else available at the time to assist him. The BC is not equipped to provide this type of emergency medical care and has other duties of managing the fire scene. He was presented with the injured firefighter, a lost fire crew, no communications, no water source, and a well-involved fire with obvious fire fatalities. He was one of the captains who lacked personal integrity mentioned earlier in my career, but he had done a good job on this fire scene.

My next assignment as a captain was at a busy single-piece station. That meant that there was only one fire truck assigned to that station. Although there were only a few females in the department, one was assigned to me. She had a reputation for not getting along well with others because she had complained about many of the same things I had just tolerated.

She ended up with a bad reputation, but she really was only speaking up about the wrongs done to her. She paid the price of not being liked or accepted in the department for doing so. I wasn't necessary liked, but I couldn't be accused of complaining about their bad behavior.

One of the other individuals assigned there was transferred because he'd instigated fights in his previous assignment. He had a reputation as a pot stirrer. The youngest firefighter had issues getting along with others. Essentially it was a shift of individuals who no one wanted or could manage.

We didn't get visits from the battalion chief assigned very often. Each person assigned there had too much to say. Now they had to compete with each other. They had to figure out a way to get along. It took a few calls to convince them they needed to rely on each other. The logistics of the station made for an environment that forced mutual cooperation and teamwork. The next arriving fire truck took several minutes to arrive to help with fire operations, so it was important that the members of our crew got along and worked well together. Over time, the experiences of working calls together improved the shift's effectiveness.

My management strategy was to allow the diversity of the crew to work through their differences. This allowed them to identify and appreciate the differences and strengths of each member. It improved the development of the depth and capabilities of our team.

Diversity in a team provides depth. It brings different perspectives and provides more options for solutions to problems. A variety of perspectives weren't embraced by the department but could be cultivated at the company level. It became the strength of our crew. The team was unique, but that is what made us a strong team. It provided me an opportunity to deal with what might be considered personnel issues.

Effort had to be made to work out our teams on scene cohesiveness. We were dispatched to a fire caused by a gas grill. The fire was contained to the grill but had started melting the vinyl siding off the house.

I was doing my customary walk around the structure and had found a gate to advance the hose line through. My crew had already torn a section of wood fence down to gain access to the rear of the structure before I could provide direction. The situation didn't warrant that level of aggressiveness. They required specific directions to maintain discipline so tasks were completed correctly. Tearing a fence down when there was another means of access was unnecessary and caused additional damage.

The odds weren't in favor of having another female on my crew. It was strategically done. The department didn't know how to manage either one of us. She was fiercely aggressive. She couldn't survive in the department if she wasn't assertive. She was also passionate. One day, she ran out on the front ramp to break up a fistfight between some high school students. No one knew it occurred. The high school had a strong gang presence, so it wasn't the safest thing to do. She required some fine-tuning. She presented some challenges that gave me a view of what it must be like to work with me. Any female who endured a career in the fire service couldn't be timid.

While assigned to this station, which was in a well-populated urban area, we were dispatched to a large brush fire. It was uncommon to have a brush fire this large in a dense neighborhood. The fire was caused by juveniles playing with fire in a field that was being cleared to build new homes. The trees were pushed together in the center of this large cleared area. There was a service road that surrounded the cleared area for access for heavy trucks. The fire was in this pile of trees.

Across the street from the access road was another line of trees and then another street and then the next neighborhood. The residents of the nearby neighborhood were concerned that the fire was going to reach their homes. There was no route of travel. The main body of fire was consuming the trees in the center of the planned neighborhood next to theirs. If an ember were to travel to start a brush fire near their area, crews could quickly put it out. That would have been the best use of our limited resources. The department lacked the resources to fight large brush fires. It was something they didn't address due to the small number of them that occurred.

If a brush fire started, it would run out of fuel at the access road. If the fire was somehow able to jump the road and catch the next group of trees on fire, the fire would have to jump another two-lane road to reach the homes in the next neighborhood.

My strategy was to let the fire burn. The contractors were planning to burn the trees once they were done clearing them anyway. The permit just hadn't been secured yet. It was the best strategy with the limited resources and personnel. The risk-benefit identified that there was nothing to save and no loss to prevent. There was a greater risk of firefighter injury and equipment damage. Instead, when the BC got there, he requested additional resources that included a helicopter, making the incident larger.

Crews stayed out all night with the fire while efforts were made to extinguish it. This included getting some brush trucks on the access road. Several got stuck. One hit a tree, and another one ripped off its side-view mirror while backing up. One truck, while attempting to pass over a tree trunk, caused the trunk to shift and injure a firefighter. Hose lines were stretched several hundred feet through the trees. The hose lines became tangled and received fire damage.

Overtime was incurred due to the length of time that was spent on the scene, and crews had to be relieved on the scene. Several other injuries occurred, resulting in lost time from work for strains and sprains. The final outcome was the fire burned to the access road as predicted and self-extinguished because there was no more fuel to burn. The outcome was the same with or without firefighting efforts. The risks had outweighed any benefits.

Our crew was now working well together. They performed smoothly at a large multifamily residential fire, accomplishing all our tasks. The apartment complex the fire was in had had several fires before. One that occurred there before hadn't gone as well, and communications were part of the problem.

It was while I was still at the technical-rescue station. I was the driver. It was during the middle of the night. The BC hadn't conducted a roll call on the tactical channel. No captain responding initiated one or tried to reach the BC. He had slept through the dispatch of the call. It is hard to think straight when you're woken up from a dead sleep.

The apartments on fire were at the end of a court. There were streets on either side of the apartments on fire that came to a point. Burning apartments could be seen, but trucks couldn't gain entry into the complex at the point where the streets met. Trucks had to drive past the burning units to the entrance of the complex. As fire units approached, they were well aware that this would be a working fire because active fire could be seen. Everyone snapped awake when they could see four apartments on fire. Speed bumps in the complex only slowed trucks' progress and increased the anxiety.

I was the driver of the first attack engine on scene. The apartments were obviously burning, so a hydrant location was identified to connect to. Sometimes when dispatched as a working fire, everyone just gets on the truck depending on the urgency of the case comments. The case comments give details the caller gives along with updates acquired. The captain looks up the hydrant location on the way. When I briefly looked at the map, the hydrant appeared to be near the end of the court. Judging distance by a symbol on a map is sometimes hard to estimate. It was a well-populated residential area, so hydrants should be no farther than five hundred feet apart.

The newly promoted captain in the cab told me to lay in from the hydrant six hundred feet from the fire. It wasn't as close as my estimation, but it was safer than passing the last hydrant. I followed his direction and used the hydrant.

When we arrived on scene, everyone jumped off the truck into action. I assisted the jump seat member in pulling the large-diameter attack-hose line off the truck. My next job was to disconnect the large-diameter supply-hose line at the closest coupling and connect it to the truck's intake. The anxious new captain radioed the volunteer firefighter who had been left at the hydrant and told him to turn the hydrant on. The driver should be the one to request the hydrant be turned on because he or she is in the best position to know if the truck is ready to receive water.

Usually the second arriving driver radios the first on-scene driver to ensure he or she is ready for water before the second driver turns on the hydrant. This avoids any confusion. The best person to answer a question about whether the attack truck is ready to receive water is the driver. That is his or her job.

I didn't hear the radio transmission to turn the hydrant on because I was busy making hose-line connections. I wasn't ready for water yet.

The outcome was the remaining hose in the bed of the truck was charged with water. The hose wasn't connected to the truck's intake yet. The hose bed became a tangled mess of giant-sized spaghetti.

The crews were quickly running out of water. The pressure coming from the hydrant made the hose in the bed of the truck heavy and almost impossible to move. The pressure coming off a hydrant averages sixty pounds but can have pressures as high as eighty pounds. Everyone now started yelling at me to get them some water. The ladder truck wanted a supply line so they could operate their ladder pipe. They had set up for an elevated defensive stream since the fire was so large.

The volunteer who had charged the hydrant realized what had happened. He was forcefully directed to go back and turn the hydrant off. He saw the damage his action of turning the hydrant on had done. He ran back as fast as he could to turn the water off.

Hydrant wrenches had to be used to break the connection since it was under water pressure. It was five-inch supply-hose line. It was so tight the connection had to be hit with a rubber mallet. When the coupling broke apart, water gushed up four feet high and hit me square in the chest and face. My knee-high leather fire boots filled with all those gallons of water.

The driver of the second engine had dressed out to fight fire since the job of securing the water for my truck had been taken care of by the volunteer. When he saw my predicament, he came over to assist me in full gear. He was able to help me drag the heavy, full, five-inch hose over to the nearest hydrant. The closest hydrant happened to be right behind my truck. Thankfully, it was closer, just as I'd thought. We hooked the already-charged hose line to the hydrant and dragged the other end over and connected it to my intake.

I now had water. Fire operations could continue. The volunteer had run back and forth several times, trying to help undo the damage that had been done when he'd turned the hydrant on. When questioned about why he'd turned the hydrant on before being asked to, he told me the captain had radioed him to turn it on. The poor guy was berated and exhausted from running back and forth. He ended up going to the hospital for dehydration and hadn't even performed any interior firefighting.

I was livid. Jokes started about my all-too-obvious charged hose bed. That is something you just can't hide. To make things worse, my leather boots were filled with water, and they started shrinking on my feet. Firefighters were allowed to purchase leather boots at their own expense and wear them, but they were not issued. They cost several hundred dollars. Because my boots were so wet from the inside out, they shrank on my feet.

Several people tried to pull them off, but they eventually had to be cut off my feet. That was the only way they could be removed. They had fit perfectly. They could have been running shoes. They fit well so I could perform any task while wearing them. This only added to my frustration. I had to go back to wearing loose-fitting rubber boots and received blisters. Every time my feet sloshed around in those rubber boots and resulted in a blister, it reminded me of that night of poor communications.

When operations are long, drivers take turns doing labor-intensive overhaul after the fire is extinguished. Wearing breathing apparatus was still required because of the deep-seated drop-down materials that were still smoldering and burning.

When I put my breathing apparatus on, it compressed the transmit button between the breathing apparatus harness strap and a wooden chock that was hanging on my coat used to prop doors open. The urgency to put the fire out was over, so the jokes about my charged hose bed began. My frustration with the captain giving the order to charge the hydrant was transmitted over the radio. That made the incident more comical. This captain took great lengths to come across as capable since he was newly promoted. His actions on this incident made him look incapable.

He directed a crew to use a hose line to douse down some burning materials inside with a hose line outside. They used a straight stream for penetration. They weren't aware of firefighters operating inside and knocked them down with the stream.

My whole response to that action and my complaint about the order to charge the hydrant was now being transmitted over the tactical channel on the radio to all the crews on the scene and anyone else listening to the fire. It wasn't very complimentary. There was also no denying who said it. I was the only female operating on the scene.

The fire chief responded to the scene because of how large the fire was. He made a point to come ask me how everything had gone on the fire. I told him I couldn't imagine him missing my critique on the radio, but I would recap it if he wanted me to. He laughed at me. What could he say? I was right and becoming more confident and obviously assertive.

CHAPTER EIGHT

Preplan

To be successful in the fire service, I needed a plan.

A fire preplan outlines the floor plan of a structure and provides a map to locate essential safety features. It gives the location of fire protection equipment and includes emergency shutoff location information. It includes special considerations that may require extra time or manpower, like residents who require assistance or can't walk.

My preplan included advancement in the department. This required me to go outside my comfort zone and learn other disciplines of the department to be an effective leader at the next level in the department.

It was exciting running calls, but a position came up in the fire-investigations division. This opportunity presented itself before I had considered and was ready to take an administrative position. There had only been a few captains who had held that position. It was a well-sought-after position for administrative work if you were willing to take an office job. Most officers stayed in the position until they either retired or were promoted. That's why the opportunity didn't come up very often.

This vacancy was only available because the male supervisor was having a sexual relationship with the female investigator he supervised, so he was being transferred out of the division.

I was a strategic thinker, and I knew depth of experience in the fire service was a desired quality for promotion, so I submitted my transfer.

I knew I could be a better leader if I became more diverse in the disciplines of the fire service. The different perspectives of different positions in the department would provide me insight to be able to benefit the department as a whole and help me to make better-informed decisions.

Fire operations are the bread and butter of the fire service, but it takes so much more to make a fire department run. Volunteering and taking assignments in the administrative functions of the fire department rounds out your level of expertise. It was a rare opportunity to become the supervisor in the fire-investigations division.

I had reservations about going in the office because my supervisor would be one of the captains I had been exposed to earlier in my career. He didn't want me to have the position about as much as I didn't want him as my supervisor. The captain tried to block my transfer, but the fire chief granted my transfer, feeling I was the best candidate for the position.

The fire chief thought I was best suited to handle the current personnel issues. I was as qualified as the other applicants and in some cases more qualified. Overheard conversations revealed the opinion that the position was granted to me because of my gender—the same reasoning I'd heard used when I was promoted. My strategy was to do a good job and prove them wrong.

There was some damage control that needed to be done. The female investigator remained in her position, and I found myself managing another one of the few females in the department.

Fire investigations consisted of a division of six officers with police powers. Two of these officers were still active on the FEMA team. After the team deployed a few times, the realization of the strain on the fire-investigations division became apparent.

The FEMA team was still important to me, especially because of the many sacrifices I'd made. To allow the two investigators the opportunity to deploy, I strategically opted to stay back and manage the fire-investigation division, which was now my responsibility, but this required me to help cover the caseload.

As the supervisor of the division, it was my responsibility to ensure it ran properly. Not everyone should leave on a deployment at the same time. This was something our fire department was never good at. The top staff in our department was never disciplined enough to stay back and run the fire department, which was their primary role. They all departed at the same time to deploy, leaving many positions within the department vacant while the team was deployed.

Most deployments consisted of the same people, although there were many other equally qualified members of the team. There was a well-known list of what was considered the top team players, and they were roistered every time. I was considered an essential member of the technical-search component.

The task force leader for the team would frequently choose friends to deploy and list them in other components they weren't trained to function in to roster them for a deployment. The technical-search component was harder to fake because it required an understanding of the listening devices and search cameras.

The same people deployed predominately out of the technical-rescue station and left the department lacking to provide local service for any calls requiring special technical-rescue assistance. Before my resignation from the FEMA team, I made sure there was someone there qualified to fill my position.

All things come to an end. I had new responsibilities relating to my new position. There are circumstances that require you to move on. It is better when you have some control over the decision. Some goals aren't attainable. I didn't feel like I was giving up, just choosing to spend my efforts on goals on which I have a bigger influence.

I had spent almost twenty years on the FEMA team, so I had given it my best effort. I felt like I had sincerely given it my best effort and still couldn't reach my goal for reasons outside my control, and I simply had to develop another strategic plan. This happens on fire scenes when the offensive attack isn't working. Crews retreat because it is the safest thing to do. The risk-benefit analysis proves the risks outweigh the benefits. The fire is still attacked, just with a different strategy. My new role and responsibility was now dedicated to the fire-investigations division.

While assigned to fire investigations, I became pregnant for the second time, which presented a dilemma. They had never had a female in fire investigations in this condition, so the department was never presented with the issue of what to do if the supervisor was pregnant. Fortunately, working through our department's human resource (HR) director, it was determined that I could remain the supervisor of the fire-investigations division. I reviewed the other fire investigators' cases. I just didn't take any cases myself during my limited-duty status.

My medical release was approved to attend an arson-investigations class while pregnant. The rest of my training was acquired five weeks after the birth of my son. The sixteen-week training was out of town. This proved challenging because I was still trying to breastfeed, so I carried a backpack, pumped milk, and stored it for the week.

I was uncomfortable during defensive tactics because of my condition. To be pushed hard and held face down on a mat was uncomfortable, but my determination was fixed to continue to nurse while out of town. To be successful, it had to be accomplished three times a day, four days a week, for sixteen weeks.

While on the shooting range, it required that a portable bathroom be used to pump. No one knew it was going on. The backpack was always with me. This is how much determination it required to fulfill my goal.

The female in the investigation division was very good at her job, but her personal life was not in accordance with the standards of her position and influenced her work. She had relationships with coworkers, individuals in other department agencies that we frequently worked with, and even some of the suspects we were investigating. This created unique challenges and involved many investigations into her conduct. Her relationship with the prior captain in fire investigations is why there was a need for a new supervisor.

My supervisor over the fire-investigations division had had a prior affair with this female investigator. He was still interested in her, although he was married. She came to me as her supervisor about complaints of his continued unwanted advances. It was my job to rectify any sexual harassment complaints as her supervisor. It was a unique situation that required me to counsel my supervisor.

The female investigator put together a program to try to rehabilitate juvenile offenders instead of just sentencing them to juvenile detention. Together, we presented the program to the city attorney's office and the judges in the juvenile criminal system. The philosophy and presentation were sound. The research into rehabilitative programs was completed. They were open to try it.

Most prosecutors were receptive to try some type of rehabilitative program instead of jail time. The program was well received. The female investigator's personal interest in these juveniles is what made the program successful. Most of the male investigators didn't place the same value on the program. The commitment to the program and the juvenile's rehabilitation is what motivated us, and that's why the program was successful. She cared, and it showed in the presentation of the program.

The rest of the investigators included a senior investigator who oftentimes said what was on his mind and wasn't always politically correct. His tactics were successful, however, on arson suspects. A female previously convicted of arson complained to me about the way he'd questioned her on a case. He had been the arresting officer in her prior arson conviction. She was a current suspect in an active arson case.

This senior investigator felt comfortable joking around with employees in other divisions in the fire services department. A fire education specialist felt like he was creating a hostile work environment. They both drove city vehicles. The senior investigator was used to driving an unmarked police car at high speeds. The fire education specialist drove an old support vehicle to transport props and fire education material to elementary schools.

He had recently participated in a defensive driving class for police officers. The bumpers on police cars are flexible and routinely used to push disabled vehicles. He pushed this educator's rear bumper as she sat at a stopped traffic light. She became extremely upset about it and filed a complaint. He had improperly used a city vehicle, and the incident could have resulted in property damage and personal injury.

He was counseled, disciplined, and directed to limit his contact with her to necessary work-related matters only.

The division was rounded out with someone who did the minimums of the job, someone who had legal problems of his own and had to be transferred out, and an investigator who needed support from the senior investigators and couldn't work independently. These were some of the personnel issues that existed upon my arrival into the division.

The legal and court systems were challenging to navigate through. There was a process to complete to carry a weapon. There was much to learn and personnel issues to manage.

An investigator who was in the division had received a driving-under-the-influence (DUI) charge and had spent the night in jail. The magistrate had called to notify me that one of the investigators was in jail and needed to be bailed out. The investigator's wife had recently left him, and he had talked about going out more at night. I initially attributed his drinking to his recent breakup. Later, it would become apparent that he was an alcoholic. He also had a drunk in public and a DUI charge in another state.

He became depressed about the obvious consequences of his actions. He was relieved of his weapon and could no longer be an active fire investigator. He ultimately lost his employment with the department.

If you are convicted of a crime yourself, you can't be a law enforcement officer. It can minimize your ability to make charges against others and potentially influence prior outcomes of cases.

The investigator asked me to go to court with him as a character witness. It appeared to be an isolated incident related to his recent separation. My supervisor also went to court on his behalf. My supervisor and I saw him at a department Christmas party between the time of this court appearance and the next court date scheduled. This investigator was drinking at the party.

He drove after drinking at this party. My supervisor didn't act on this knowledge. I went to the prosecuting commonwealth attorney and withdrew my character witness testimony based on the realization he had a problem. It wasn't an isolated case. He was an alcoholic and wasn't going to stop drinking and driving. He was a danger to himself and others.

My supervisor was unwilling to do the same. The decision to go to the prosecuting attorney with information that would result in his termination was hard for me, because the man was liked and a good investigator. The other fire investigators had seen him at the same party and knew it was the right thing to do, but it still felt as though I was breaking an oath of loyalty to the division.

Nonetheless, my conscience wouldn't allow me to sacrifice my personal integrity. My actions weren't popular. He had broken the law and was now going to pay the price.

It was a bench trial. All people involved in the case raised their arms and swore to tell the truth. Everyone stood before the judge and took turns answering questions. I was surprised when my supervisor said under oath that he didn't know about any prior drinking charges.

When he gave his response that he didn't know about any prior drinking charges, my head jerked around to look at him in disbelief. Apparently, he didn't want to look negligent for having knowledge about the investigators drinking and not acting on it. His statement really had no bearing on the investigator being convicted of DUI or not. Our statements had more to do with letting the judge know he would be fired if he received a conviction.

The judge saw my response and shook his head. He smiled at me. He wasn't there to hear a perjury case against a city official. The case was about the investigator's DUI. If the judge pursued it, many prior cases ending in convictions regarding building violations would be in question due to the integrity of the fire marshal presenting them.

I knew my supervisor had information that this fire investigator had been stopped for suspicion of DUI before. He had been released to his battalion chief in fire operations and not charged. The incident had been believed to be isolated then, too, so no charges had been filed, and no action was taken.

The investigator was found guilty of DUI and received a conviction. He appealed the ruling but lost the appeal. He lost his job with the department. My supervisor wasn't supportive during this incident.

There were still physical challenges to my new position in fire investigations. Some suspects had a known history of resisting arrest. One of these cases involved a suspect who was in the hospital and had sustained burns while lighting a fire. Another fire investigator and I questioned the suspect while he was still in the hospital.

The suspect had threatened to kill his grandmother he lived with. A drug user, he had been physically abusing her, so she asked him to move out. He'd left after she'd had to call the police because he had been beating her for asking him to move out. Later that night while she was asleep, he'd come back and lit the house on fire. He'd set the fire in the garage, thinking the crime of arson would be covered up by all the potential things that could start a fire in a garage.

The suspect had used an accelerant. He'd poured a lot of gasoline throughout the garage. He hadn't anticipated the gas vapors from the gasoline would flash and catch on fire when he lit the match. He'd received burns on his hands and face as a result. His hair and eyebrows had been burned. His burns had been severe enough that he'd had to be transported to the hospital.

His story was that he had just come back to get a few things out of the house in the middle of the night so his grandmother wouldn't see him as there was an active restraining order for him not to go near her. He said he didn't know how the fire started. His version of the story included seeing a spark in the garage. He bragged it was good he had come back to the house and detected the fire. He said he'd saved his grandmother's life.

He said all he remembered was seeing the flicker of the flame by the hot-water heater in the garage. Their hot-water heater was electric, so it didn't have a pilot light like gas hot-water heaters.

We were questioning him again, but we already had sufficient cause to arrest him. He had a history of resisting arrest. My planned tactic if he resisted arrest was to rip off his bandages and dig into his burns. Burns are extremely painful, and this tactic would have a high degree of success for gaining compliance with my requests. Digging into a drug addict's burns who had tried to kill his grandmother didn't cause me much mental conflict.

The actual work the division did was professional and fulfilling. I formed close relationships with the police department, bomb squad, commonwealth attorney's office, and others in the judicial system. The discipline issues presented while in fire investigations prepared me for bigger personnel issues later.

The division included the responsibility to manage investigators who carried weapons and had arrest powers—investigators sometimes acted like juveniles themselves. There were routine complaints from parents stemming from their children's arrest and subsequent court-ordered attendance in the Fire Arson Course for Teens program.

My assignment in investigations gave me perspective on how children's environments can have an influence on children's future fire-setting behavior. A particularly troubling case involved a habitual arson offender who'd started setting fires as a juvenile.

The percentage of true pyromaniacs is small. This case included textbook qualifiers. He was male and a social loner. He struggled emotionally with how to live with his same-sex attraction. It had started as a fascination with fire as a juvenile that grew to an addiction outside his control.

He started burning with paper, then leaves and grass. He would make false calls for fires and bomb scares. While talking with local community college department heads about the fire science curriculum including an arson class, he saw us. He was at a bus transfer station on campus waiting for his bus connection.

He was familiar to us. He called in a bomb threat because the opportunity presented itself. The school's buildings had to be evacuated. The bomb squad conducted a search of the buildings. He was standing in the crowd watching. It excited him.

When approached, he was visibly excited to see us. He particularly liked to talk to me and the other female investigator. He really enjoyed what he called our "girl talk." He would wander around his neighborhood wearing women's clothing. He'd started out setting brush fires but had escalated to burning vacant houses around his neighborhood. He left some mail addressed to him inside a vacant house that he set on fire. He wanted to be caught and sent to jail.

Right after getting out of jail, he broke into a commercial structure. He took some candy and petty cash. He triggered the smoke alarm by setting a small fire in a trashcan. He then waited for the police to arrive.

He was dressed in a bikini with a long boa scarf and high heels. He was excited to go back to jail. That is where he felt the most comfortable because it provided him an opportunity to live the lifestyle he was too conflicted to live. He was diagnosed with AIDS and sent to prison to serve out a long sentence. I never saw him again.

Other fires included a fire in an abandoned building that resulted in a fire fatality. The building had actually burned the night before. The fire was thought to have started due to a lightning strike. The house was fully involved when the first fire unit's arrived. The roof had collapsed, and all that stood were the outside walls. The house was vacant and had burned before. The house had been scheduled to be torn down for new construction. Due to the condition of the building, crews did not perform an interior search that night.

The next day, the station received another call for the house because the fire had rekindled and started burning again. It had never been fully extinguished the night before. There were many layers of debris trapped under the roof. These materials had smoldered throughout the night and caught on fire the next day. When fire crews responded, they started digging through the debris to find the hidden fire because they didn't want another rekindle.

While they were digging through the layers of debris, they found a body. The body was heavily charred. At first, it looked like he had been shot in the head, but the coroner determined his skull had ruptured from pressure caused by boiling fluids and organs. The hole was the pressure seeking an escape.

The investigation identified he was homeless and had been living in the abandoned structure, which did not have a working smoke detector. A smoke detector identifies fires in their early stages and gives occupants a chance to escape.

He had found a place to sleep out of the weather. His bike was nearby. Our investigation revealed he had been staying there awhile. A backpack and a few of his belongings were found nearby where he perished in the fire. It looked as if he was trying to get his bike out of the house because he was found tangled up in it. An old identification card was found in his backpack, and his sister was contacted. When questioned why she hadn't reported him missing, she stated that he'd routinely gone missing for several months and his homelessness had made it hard to contact him.

I was amazed at how little some people valued life. One fire victim was found in a burning dumpster, the body wrapped in a carpet. The victim had been shot in the head, and the fire had been set to try to hide his identity and destroy the evidence of the murder.

One murder occurred over drugs. Both parties were in their twenties. The seller came to the home of the one purchasing the drugs. After the drugs were received, he didn't have the money to pay for them, so they got into a fistfight over payment.

The sister of the seller called the police to report her brother missing. She knew where he had gone. When he didn't come back, she went over there. When she saw his car, she knocked on the door. When no one answered the door, she called the police and gave them the address and told them about the drug deal.

When the police arrived, the suspect wouldn't open the door, and the police SWAT team had to make entry to the house. Right before they tried to make entry, the suspect set the house on fire. During his confession of the murder, he denied the arson. The murder had a longer sentence. He was charged with capital murder because it was committed during a felony robbery. Capital murder could result in the death penalty.

It took some candy bars the following day to get his confession to the arson. When the SWAT team made entry, he'd started the fire with the welding torch he used at work. He wouldn't have been able to survive the fire. He wouldn't have been able to breathe. He'd lived there alone, so it was hard to deny knowing about a dead body in the bathtub when the SWAT team entered.

The buyer had no prior criminal history. He was a little older and stronger. He had become addicted to drugs, and his addiction to the drugs was strong enough to kill to get them.

He described in graphic detail how he had beat the other man to death. He was casual in his description, never showing any remorse. It sounded as though he believed it was the seller's fault because he'd insisted on receiving money for the drugs he'd delivered that the arsonist didn't have money for but needed.

The arsonist said the drug dealer just wouldn't stay down after he'd knocked him out. He had to continually beat him to keep him from getting back up. He described how he wrapped his head in plastic and taped it around the neck because his head was bleeding so profusely and he didn't want to get the carpet bloody. The arsonist didn't take responsibility for his own actions that resulted in the drug dealer's death, and he repeated his frustration that the guy wouldn't stay down, so he'd had to keep hitting him.

He said he was surprised he hadn't suffocated in the plastic shower curtain. He said he'd been tired of listening to him moan, so he'd carried him in the plastic and put him in the bathtub. He said that if we gave him something to eat he would tell us what happened. He gave his confession for the price of a Big Mac meal from McDonald's. He was asked to repeat parts of his statement because it was hard to hear him over the rattle of the paper the food was wrapped in and because his mouth was full of food while he talked.

In another case we investigated, I learned that revenge could motivate people to do hideous things. We responded to a case involving arson to cover a double homicide. A man paid someone to kill his estranged wife. They had a child together that lived with the mother but was visiting the father out of the state. The man wanted custody of the child and didn't want to continue paying child support.

She had another child from a prior relationship. She was home with this child when she was shot and killed as she opened the front door. The child was shot and killed as he slept on the couch by the front door. The dog was shot, and the phone lines were cut. Then the killer started a fire in the kitchen.

They were good at shooting people but were poor fire starters. The fire was small and self-extinguished. The gunfire alerted the neighbors, who called the police. The smoke from the fire prevented police officers from entering the structure. They called the fire department to put out the fire first. The fire department didn't want to go inside until the police department had secured the residence to ensure the gunman wasn't still in the house.

While the two departments discussed a strategy, the fire burned itself out. The police entered the house and cleared the building. Then the fire department came in to check for fire extension. The fire hose was dragged through the building. This displaced the evidence. The bullet casings were moved from their initial placement. It made evidence collection and crime reenactment challenging. The prime suspect was the ex-husband, but because he had an alibi and the hired shooter was never found, the case was never resolved.

Having physical proof that someone started a fire makes the case easier to prove in court. My time in fire investigations taught me how far people would go to achieve their goals. Sometimes motivations are basic, like the need to eat. I watched a security video one time of someone throwing a Molotov cocktail through the window of a bar. They were trying to gain access to the money inside the bar. They took money and liquor. They were homeless. They were hungry and had a drinking problem.

There was a homeless population nearby who lived in tents in the woods. People living in desperate conditions will do unpredictable things. Most of them carried knives for protection. They were protective of the few possessions they owned. Many of them suffered from mental illnesses.

One arson case involved a man who suffered from hallucinations. He lived with his parents. He felt as if there were bugs crawling on him in bed while he slept, so he set the bed on fire while he was still in it. The fire spread to the rest of the house. Firefighters had to rescue him. Mentally handicapped patients are hard to place. There may not be room for them in mental facilities. No homeless shelters want them if they had a history of arson, for fear of the safety of other occupants. They needed help they couldn't receive in jail, but because of these concerns, that was exactly where they ended up. This man was no different.

The tenured investigator took this suspect into custody and couldn't find placement for him, so he was taking him to jail. The investigator felt sorry for the man who was scared and complaining of the tightness of the handcuffs. Protocol, when a suspect comes into the intake area of the jail, is that the suspect remains handcuffed. They are even handcuffed to a bench if left unattended.

They remain handcuffed even when sitting in front of the magistrate who listens to the case to determine if there is enough evidence to issue a warrant for an arrest. The suspect is brought to sit in front of the magistrate with the arresting officer behind a bulletproof window. Because the investigator didn't feel he was dangerous and felt empathy for him, he took the suspects handcuffs off prematurely. When they were sitting in front of the magistrate, the suspect became agitated and punched the investigator in the side of the face. The magistrate saw the punch coming but couldn't warn the investigator fast enough. It was another lesson learned to follow the rules and not cut corners.

Fire fatalities involving children are sometimes the hardest to work. I went to visit a mother in the hospital recovering from burns. She was separated from her mentally ill husband. She had a thirteen-year-old son. She had fallen asleep downstairs, and when she woke up, she found her house on fire. There was heavy fire upstairs where her son was sleeping. She had tried to make her way upstairs to wake him, but she was unable to make it up the stairs due to the large amount of heat and flames.

She was driven outside by the high heat and smoke, but she still received burns so severe that several of her fingers burned off. One of her fingers was found in the front yard. When fire units responded, she was in the backyard screaming her son's name. He succumbed to the smoke and flames. The fire was ruled an arson. Her estranged husband had hired someone to kill them.

When I visited her in the hospital during the investigation, I asked her to recount the events of the evening the fire occurred. When she got to the point in the story that she realized she couldn't reach her son, she started crying and screaming. She did so with such agony of soul that I will never forget it.

There was a triple fire fatality involving two children that occurred on Christmas Day. My own children wouldn't have me home this Christmas morning. The scene at the house fire included a Santa letter along with untouched milk and cookies. It was an eerie sight. It no longer seemed like a sacrifice that I would miss that particular Christmas morning with my own children. They were alive. There is nothing quite like the sight of a dead mother and child by a Christmas tree in the charred remains of what used to be their home. They had to be identified by their jewelry and what they were wearing.

We stayed with the bodies until the medical examiner arrived. The fire units had cleared the scene. It was shift change. One shift had worked Christmas Eve and had the fire. They would be able to go home to their families. The other shift was coming in on Christmas Day and had already had an early Christmas morning with their children.

The cause of the fire was due to unattended decorative candles. Other contributing factors were alcohol and a lack of operating smoke detectors. They had not done anything criminal. They had been drinking responsibly in their own home. They didn't know their smoke detector batteries were dead. Candles are pretty that time of year, and they never dreamed they would end up being the cause of lost hopes and dreams.

My perspective changed while in fire investigations. I learned the intricate details of people's lives and learned the influence that events had leading up to the accident. I learned who they were as people. They became real.

It was harder to work cases knowing more details about the people involved. In the station running emergency calls, there is a safe distance between your initial response to the call and the final outcome. You get called in an emergency. You respond to the initial need for help. You can then go back to the station without getting too personally involved.

A common practice for emergency workers is to joke around after calls to relieve stress and pressure of the gravity of the things they had witnessed, but this was harder to do when you became more personally involved with the people during an investigation.

Although I enjoyed my assignment in fire investigations, there was an opportunity for promotion to battalion chief. My husband working in the department was being transferred to a services day position. To avoid conflicts with child care, I participated in the promotional process for battalion chief.

I was qualified, had completed a master's degree, and had the experience of fire operations and services. Our new fire chief who came from outside the department promoted me. He told me when he promoted me that he wasn't making many people happy by promoting me but that he had confidence in my abilities and the promotion was deserved.

After my promotion to battalion chief, I was transferred to one of the busiest battalions in the department that included the marine specialty division. The police department had marine resources as well. The relationships formed while pursuing my master's degree and while working in fire investigations continued back out in fire operations. My responsibilities as a battalion chief in fire operations included running marine calls with the police department marine resources. Certain types of calls like bomb threats required the police and fire department to work together, so my associations with the police department continued.

CHAPTER NINE

Communications

After my promotion, I represented our department as the public information officer (PIO), the spokesperson for the department. On large emergency events, the PIO worked with the local news to provide details so they could report on incidents.

News crews all wanted to run breaking stories. To accomplish this, they utilized various tactics. They tried to become your best friend to receive favors, and they followed you everywhere. My size-up was that correct reporting would be beneficial to the fire department. I recognized the need to educate the public on the benefits of smoke detectors and potential fire causes. To remain fair and impartial, I utilized a voice message system that notified all media at the same time, and I posted on Twitter. The voice message could be played with any video clip they got from the scene. The relationship between the media and the department was not well established but improved as information was provided that was fair, thorough, and timely.

I learned what the media wanted to report on by interacting with them. I provided the basic information along with what they would want to know next. Rarely did I receive additional questions about an incident from the media. They usually had follow-up questions. I became a better PIO as I anticipated what questions would be asked and was ready to answer them.

Basic questions asked included information about when the fire department received the call, when they arrived, what the conditions were when the trucks arrived, how long it took to put the fire out, and whether smoke detectors were present. Always of concern was whether anyone was hurt during the incident, including the firefighters who responded. The number one question was what had caused the fire.

The cause of a fire can't always be determined right away. It may take further investigation. Materials gathered at the incident are sent off to a laboratory to confirm the presence of flammable liquids. An investigator interviews all the parties involved. The investigation might be criminal in nature. Suspicions of arson require secrecy to make involved parties comfortable talking to the investigator. The fire-cause determination is never quick enough for the media, who are trying to make a breaking news discovery.

The more forthcoming with information, the fewer the number of phone calls received from the media. No news station got any more or less information than the other. If there was an update, it was put out to all parties at the same time. This method of sharing information was efficient and fair.

There were times the news crew wanted to do a live broadcast, which required quick responses to tough questions. It was a breaking news story on live television, so it was supposed to elicit excitement.

The media could be frustrating. They only wanted to cover the blood and gore of an incident, looking for shock value and drama, but the people involved already had enough drama.

When offered upbeat stories about current fire recruit academies, canine training, and FEMA rescue classes designed to improve victim's survival, they were rarely interested.

A case involving a juvenile planning an assault on his school was forefront in the news. They wanted to know all the details of the case, including the identity of the suspect. The suspect was a juvenile whose identity was protected, but they pushed for the information anyway.

During my first assignment as the PIO, a question came up from the media that had internal exposure problems to the fire department. They were questioning the validity of some current fire officer's college degrees. There were some external exposure problems for the city HR department. The question was about whether the degrees were from accredited universities.

A story broke about the fire department's acceptance of nonaccredited degrees for eligibility to participate in promotional processes. It was a valid concern because the city paid members a higher salary for having a college degree. My choice of curriculum from an accredited university had been a good one. Many other firefighters were playing catch-up because they hadn't started their educations early enough, including some of the higher ranking officers.

I was able to tell the media that my degree was from an accredited university, but I was unable to comment on what everyone else's education level may be. My exposures were covered. I referred them to the city's HR department to confirm the degrees of other members of the department. HR regulated the tuition reimbursement and educational incentive pay. They would have the records of what members in the city had degrees that they were paying educational incentive for and had reimbursed members for tuition.

The records could be requested under the Freedom of Information Act (FOIA). They could then compare the people on the tuition incentive list and list of officers in the fire department and make a comparison. It was a way to stay politically correct without negatively commenting on the status of some of the department members' educational levels, but be able to answer their questions.

My PIO duties continued on nights and weekends when transferred back to fire services, but it was time to run calls again.

My first shift back in fire operations I responded to a second-alarm multifamily residential fire.

It was time to take command.

Strong incident command systems maintain control of crews working on the scene and keep personal accountability reports. I would be the second arriving battalion chief to this fire. My job was to assist the first arriving battalion chief and handle personal accountability passports of the firefighters. The system requires a personal accountability report (PAR) every time a unit gives a status. This is an accountability system to ensure firefighters aren't lost or missing. The incident commander can call for PARs any time during the incident. They are utilized when a fire transitions from interior to exterior to ensure all crews are accounted for.

Each firefighter carries a nameplate with his or her name on it that is stuck with Velcro to the firefighter's helmet. At the beginning of each shift, the fire officer on the unit takes the names of each firefighter assigned to his or her unit and builds a passport with those members' names on it to identify their unit.

The officer during a fire brings that passport to the battalion chief's vehicle. The battalion chief then manages the passports. The battalion has a visual reminder of what units are on scene and available for assignment. The BC can use the passports to help keep track of where the units are working. When the battalion chief gets status reports about working fire unit's progress, the PAR is given. The PAR is then checked with the passport to ensure there are no missing firefighters or units.

The first arriving BC is in command. He or she is really busy, especially in the initial stages of a fire. The second BC comes in to handle the PARs and accountability of working units, which is what I anticipated would be my job. When fires aren't going well or are large enough, though, they expand and result in the second battalion chief taking command of a division.

The strategy used by the BC in charge wasn't working well. The fire was getting larger, so it was time for me as the second arriving battalion chief to move forward and manage a division. My division included interior fire-attack operations. The fire had started in a middle unit townhouse and quickly spread to the units on both adjoining sides of it. Divisions can be set up exterior or on one of the sides.

Access had been gained to the other units, and all three units involved in the fire could be entered from the rear. I was inside one of the fire units with a crew when a hose stream operated by someone outside hit us. I gave an order on the radio for the hose line to be shut down. Before a hose line is directed inside a structure, it has to be coordinated with operating crews inside. Interior crews can be hit with the hose stream, or the stream coming in can cause steam conversion and result in burns to interior operating crews.

The person operating the hose line was the fire chief. He was wrong to direct a hose stream inside where crews were operating. He was the recipient of the reprimand I delivered over the radio. He was wrong to do it, but it presented a unique situation because he was the fire chief.

My first shift back in operations was memorable because of the working fire and because of the reprimand I gave to the fire chief. Radio communications should be clear and concise. It makes the message clear. My message was clear and received.

The main duty of an operational battalion chief is to provide command and control of emergency scenes. Large fires requiring a BC to move forward into a division are not as common. I had encountered one of those rare occasions on my first shift within the first few hours.

This was a different fire chief, but I became acquainted with all of them. He had been worried about the fire spread, so he'd picked up a hand line that was left in the backyard and started trying to knock some fire down. He had not been involved in firefighting for quite some time, and he had forgotten some basic tactics and strategies. But he was still the fire chief. His position presented a dilemma in asking him to follow the same rules.

His duties were focused on administrative work. I'm sure he wanted to ensure he didn't look bad as the fire chief if there was a large fire loss. I was forming a reputation for speaking up when something wasn't going well. As a firefighter, my attempts were quickly squashed. Each new rank achieved resulted in my becoming more vocal.

I was finally in the right position to do so. I would later learn that speaking up wasn't always appreciated. This was especially true if it was embarrassing to a senior officer. It didn't matter how right I may be.

During my time working in fire operations, my captains were given the parameters and expectations to accomplish the job, and then they were left to work independently. I felt this was the best way to instill confidence in them, giving them the opportunity to expand their knowledge base. I provided input if something wasn't going well or wasn't being done as requested. My actions communicated trust and confidence in them.

The fire chief wasn't comfortable with that style leadership, and his senior staff managed the same way he did. This created a micromanagement style of leadership that impeded progress in even simple tasks.

As an example, the fire chief showed up to one of my commercial fires since he lived nearby. His response was expected, although not necessary. He was the fire chief, so he had the prerogative to show up to any call he felt like coming to. It was still surprising to see him show up to many routine cases.

Firefighting shouldn't become routine, or it breeds complacency, but it was our job, and the crews were proficient at fire operations. Some cases presented unique challenges, and there was always something to be learned from each case. His job as the fire chief was not to respond to fires unless they were large scale or catastrophic.

As the fire chief, he had many other duties that needed to be handled. He had been promoted through the ranks too quickly to have attained the required level of competency. By responding to unnecessary calls, it appeared he was not comfortable in his new role as fire chief. He appeared to lack confidence in his new responsibilities and projected his lack of confidence to fire crews, making it appear as if he lacked trust in the fire crew's abilities.

His lack of confidence in his abilities was projected on fire crews when he responded to every call. The outcome was that crews felt as if the chief didn't trust their abilities. Unfortunately, his presence became a negative thing.

On my particular incident, fire operations were going smoothly. When he arrived on scene, he was excited. It is hard to wait for a fire to go out as a chief. Orders are given, but it takes time to accomplish the tasks.

Safety precautions have to be followed on a fire scene. The process wasn't moving quickly enough for him. Fire operations sometimes take discipline and patience. The strategy has to have a chance to work. Watching from outside makes time move slowly. Status reports are hard to wait for. Nothing ever moves fast enough when you are the one waiting.

He wanted me to constantly ask for updates. He wanted me to give specific instruction for the ladder crew to ladder the building. It was their standard practice and already in progress. There was a general opinion by senior officers that firefighters had to be told to do everything, which is a by-product of their micromanagement style of leadership. They thought it showed command presence by the officer to talk the fire out.

I kept radio transmissions clear and concise, just what was necessary and required. If it was an order given for a tactic to support the strategy, it was relayed. If it was a status or accountability check, it was transmitted. If it was relevant information for fire crews and necessary to maintain control and accountability of crews working, then it was communicated. If it was unnecessary lengthy transmissions that added nothing to the incident, I avoided them.

Once the ladder was placed, I communicated its presence and location. By taking this management approach with crews, they reciprocated respect to me. I received respect from the fire crews that worked for me but not from the people I worked for.

The projection of their insecurities on emergency scenes made me critique my actions. It helped me be critical of my decisions and make improvements. Senior chiefs continued the cycle of trying to control fire scenes, which was something they felt more comfortable managing.

On this fire, crews were having trouble accessing a rear metal door. The fire chief continued to make comments and suggestions that were distracting. His ideas had already been tried. He didn't like my confidence in the crew's abilities.

My crews had proven to make good decisions on incidents, so they were trusted. As an example, one officer in my battalion who was dispatched to a residential fire alarm encountered a bedroom fire upon his arrival. There was fire blowing out the bedroom window. The occupant was outside waiting for them and confirmed she was the only one who lived there. He correctly decided to upgrade the case to a working fire. Other fire units were dispatched to the call, but there would be a delay in their arrival.

He used good judgment to remain outside and fight the fire defensively until other fire units arrived. This was a good decision because they didn't have any backup if something had gone wrong. There was a department two-in-two-out policy that specifies interior firefighting should only occur if there are two people outside as backup.

An exception to the two-in-two-out rule is if there is a known or reasonable suspicion that there is an occupant inside. If someone is inside, it's expected that the firefighters would go inside to locate and rescue a trapped fire victim. This was not the case on this incident. The occupant was outside talking to the officer.

Even though this was a good call, this officer still heard negative comments from other officers. One of the officers who disagreed would go on to receive formal discipline. That officer stated he would have gone in. This would have been against policy and good judgment, but he routinely confirmed he had poor judgment. This required me to manage him differently. He was very proactive training with his crew, but he had poor judgment on limits. One of his training drills planned was to practice fire operations in a nursing home. The concept of the drill was good, but he wanted to fill the nursing home with smoke from a smoke machine.

The smoke he wanted to use is nontoxic, the same type they use in theater or for Halloween props. The problem is the residents wouldn't know that. Our senses can deceive us. If the elderly saw smoke, they could start having symptoms of breathing difficulty. They may get excited and suffer some type of cardiac event just from the excitement of seeing smoke.

Most of the elderly residents at the facility were already on oxygen or suffered from some sort of cardiac-related illness. The drill he wanted to conduct had the potential to turn into a real emergency. He didn't understand that. He proceeded to protest that he was denied permission to conduct the drill.

One particular incident demonstrated how the power of suggestion works on people. The case involved a dairy that made ice cream and manufactured dairy products. They had freezers and cooling units that separated the dairy products.

A fire inspector had recognized a leak in one of their processing units and called the case in. A full response, including a hazardous materials unit, responded. A preschool was about five hundred feet from this commercial structure. When the preschool workers saw the hazmat unit arrive, they started complaining of feeling light-headed and sick.

The unit had just been inspected. The inspector and occupant knew about the leak. They had done testing and determined that the leak was not presenting any health or safety issue due to the small amount leaking. Leakages like this are common for these types of units. Our hazmat unit confirmed this, and the business was allowed to stay open.

The hazmat team wanted to practice making an entry in their hazardous-level suits, which are only utilized with the most dangerous types of leaking product. They were utilized not because the product was hazardous but to fulfill a training requirement to make an entry wearing these suits each year. The incident was used as a drill. But when the preschool workers saw them putting on these suits, their bodies responded to the perceived threat of something hazardous, and they started complaining of real symptoms, without any real threat being present.

When they were told the building was clear and nothing was hazardous, they immediately felt better. Their preschool had been a consideration right from the beginning. The chemical properties were known. The type of chemical and amount leaking presented no hazard to them. The potential for threat to them had been identified but ruled out.

My original instructions were for them to stay inside and not take the children outside until a confirmation could be made about the product.

When senior-staff officers heard radio communications about a hazardous entry on the radio, they were mad they hadn't been notified. They started an investigation. They made assumptions about operations on an emergency scene. They jumped to conclusions without having all the facts. They did not extend courtesy or respect to others, although they demanded it themselves.

Another incident involving the captain with poor judgment occurred while he was conducting a drill using the aerial ladder to perform an elevated rescue. The error occurred when both sections of the aerial device were used as an anchor. They used the ladder as a winch to raise a load. This requires the aerial ladder to extend and retract. Because the anchor was tied around the static part of the ladder and the operating part was moving, it caused the two sections of the ladder to pull the anchor in tension in opposite directions.

The two-inch webbing and carabineer were stronger than the welds on the aerial device, so the rung was pulled off. Accidents can happen during dangerous operations. This officer didn't learn from his mistakes.

He needed a lot of counseling and received a lot of discipline. He usually got in trouble when I was off on leave. He took a crew on a roof of a business one weekend to talk about roof construction. Policy states that before you go on someone's private property you should obtain permission. He didn't do it.

To make the training seem more real, he had his crew take all the tools they would normally carry to make a hole in the roof to conduct roof ventilation. He was carrying a shepherd's hook. It has a claw on one end and a hook on the other. The roof was a rubber-membrane flat roof. He was using the tool as a walking stick and poked a hole in the rubber membrane. The rubber membrane seals a roof. If there is a hole in the material, the roof can leak.

After the incident happened, he asked his crew not to say anything about it. The crew was uncomfortable with the request, and they became more uneasy because of the roof damage, but he asked them to deny it had happened.

There had already been someone from his crew who had asked for a transfer because he was uncomfortable with the decisions this captain made. The firefighter was trying to get promoted, and he didn't want to be involved in the type of activities this captain engaged in that resulted in several administrative hearings.

Administrative hearings are formal fact-finding hearings where parties are called in to give facts of an incident. They are formal and conducted because something serious has occurred. They usually indicate discipline is warranted.

An administrative hearing was conducted because the officer had lied about the roof incident. He had been threatening the firefighters on the truck if they told the truth. It is a department offense to lie, even though senior officers had been known to. If they lied, they would go from just being witnesses to the event to being in trouble themselves.

After receiving discipline for lying, he cut up a vehicle at the training center reserved for another crew and denied doing it. He had a problem telling the truth. He lacked integrity. He worshiped senior staff. He was emulating their behavior, so he was confused when he received discipline.

He became one of my pet projects. I spent a lot of time and effort working on improvement plans and administering discipline. He was entitled to grieve his discipline, so I had to spend time listening to his complaints. It was a poor use of my time.

He was involved in the new-hire physical-agility testing. He was physically fit, but he went beyond his authority. He gave applicants special privileges that were only found out about later. Special treatment could invalidate the whole physical-agility test. He was no longer permitted to help the department in the new-hire process.

Later when I transferred out of the battalion, senior staff tried to transfer this captain with me. The fire chief threatened to fire him at one point. He couldn't go to my new assignment. His discipline prevented him from performing the duties there. He would later be promoted despite the reprimands and suspensions administered to him, only to be demoted two levels later in his career. The city policy said that a person shouldn't be promoted if they had active discipline in their personnel file, but the fire chief promoted him anyway. He represented the style of leadership they expected.

There were eight officers to supervise in my battalion, two of whom were involved in special operations. The fires that were responded to were less time consuming and challenging than managing these captains.

The station where I and the other shifts battalion chief slept had an ongoing shift war between the three shifts. The initial conflict was about whether the straight or fog tip should stay on the end of the aerial ladder. Then it expanded to what equipment should stay on the truck. The ladder crew on one shift wanted to take the high-rise equipment off the truck. They didn't think making a connection with high-rise hose was a ladder company's job.

The ladder truck routinely ran fire calls when the engine was out on a call. The ladder trucks the city bought all carried water and had pumps, with the exception of the tiller truck at the oceanfront. One day the ladder was dispatched to a call for a car fire in a parking garage. They didn't have the right equipment to make the connection to the fire protection system.

Policy outlined a standardized equipment list of what equipment should be on a vehicle. Taking this equipment off the truck violated the policy.

My shift was instructed to follow policy and leave the equipment on the truck. If they wanted to make a change, they would have to forward a written request to do so as stated in the policy. My shift remained neutral in the shift battle.

During this battle of equipment placement on the truck, beds in the bunkrooms were relocated and had to be moved back and forth as the shifts changed. It was a petty thing to demonstrate displeasure with another shift's position on the matter.

I talked to the other BCs and told them our shift was going to follow policy. I suggested they take their issues up through the chain of command.

The fighting escalated. One of the other shifts used the master-stream device in a drill and directed its stream into the bushes where some feral cats lived. The result was that several kittens were killed. It was significant because the other shift was feeding the cats and had made these cats pets. One shift shouldn't have been feeding cats, but the other shift shouldn't have inflicted intentional harm on the cats. After the kittens were killed, the other shift called PETA to conduct an investigation.

During the investigation, all the cats were caught and removed. A sign remains to this day warning people in the neighborhood behind the fire station not to feed stray cats. It was simple on our shift. They weren't to feed, catch, or kill any cats.

I responded to a wide variety of calls while in fire operations. The marine division was in my battalion. Marine operations presented special challenges. The beginning of the marine program started out with donated or acquired boats. When a new boat was purchased, the old engines were taken off the old boat and used on the new boat. There wasn't budget money committed to the program to support the purchase of new engines for the new boat. The engines were old and not large enough for the new boats to perform efficiently. Because of this, the fireboat was frequently out of service for maintenance.

On one of the days the fireboat was out of service, there was a boat fire under the bridge at the opening of the inlet to the bay. The only other boats available were rubber surf-entry boats acquired from the military, with no fire pumps. They were used primarily for waterborne rapid intervention teams (RIT) for other crews working on vessels or to actually rescue swimmers in the water. They had a quick response and could be inflated quickly. The marine division left two of these boats inflated, with motors to respond quickly. At the time, they were the only resource available when the fireboat was out of service.

These rubber boats were dispatched to rescue anyone on board a boat on fire. Fire units responded to the bridge to access the boat by land because the fireboat was out of service, and the only boats available were these rubber Zodiac boats. Hose lines had to be stretched and run off portable pumps off the beach. The situation was not ideal.

The boat was used for rescue calls. One day, it was dispatched to assist a cruise ship that had a patient onboard who needed transport to the hospital. The patient wasn't stable enough to be picked up by the coast guard and ride in their aerial stretcher. The cruise ship was coming in close enough to the bay for our fireboat to pick up the patient for transport to an ambulance at the marina so the patient could be transferred to the hospital.

The fireboat crew had to climb a rope ladder to access the side of the ship. Then a lower opening would become the transfer point to pass the patient from the ship to the fireboat. The fireboat was tethered to the ship but still bobbing in the water during the transfer of the patient. The conditions made the transfer complicated and challenged rescue workers.

Another cruise ship full of passengers became grounded in the intercoastal waterway. The ship was leaking fuel in the water, which generated a hazard. It was going to be a long operation, so all the passengers had to disembark the ship. They had to transfer from one boat to another. The fireboat was dispatched to assist.

My area also included the bridge tunnel coming into and leaving our city. A large tractor trailer of processed chickens caught fire on the twenty-three-mile bridge with two underwater tunnels that spanned the bay. The fireboat was utilized as a water source for units working on the bridge. The tractor trailer had to be towed off the bridge. Traffic was limited to one side. The fire units had to back several miles off the bridge when the call was over.

Our city experienced many violent thunderstorms throughout the summer. It was nature's way of cooling the high temperatures that resulted from the cooler ocean air meeting warmer air coming in from the west. Units might run in excess of thirty calls during a few hours. Many calls would have to hold as there weren't enough units to respond to all the calls. Calls would have to be prioritized. Modified responses were made, and only full responses of fire units were dispatched to actual reports of smoke and flames visible.

During these times, I prioritized the calls and rerouted units. There might have been several working incidents at the same time. One particularly busy day in my response area, there was a working house fire, a person pinned in a vehicle due to an accident, and a hotel fire at the same time.

Once the fire in the hotel was knocked down and under control, I cleared units from that case to go to the residential fire. Normally I wouldn't do this, but there were limited resources to handle the call volume. It took remaining units on scene longer to complete all the operations. A check for fire extension, ventilation, and the securing of utilities to isolate the fire units without shutting the whole hotel down had to be completed.

On another night with thunderstorms, a call came in across the water from a residence. The residence was located by the flames visible. It was an old farmhouse that had been renovated and was being lived in, but no one was home. The farmland had been converted into a golf course. The fire was fully involved, with every part of the house involved in fire. The house had been struck by lightning, and the fire had burned for a long time before anyone detected it.

The closest hydrant was over three thousand feet away. Each fire engine carries one thousand feet of hose. Three fire engines worth of hose had to be stretched and laid to connect the water from the hydrant to the fire engine conducting the fire attack.

A tanker was used during this process. Access to the house was limited to a golf cart path. A lock was cut off the gate to allow a fire truck to get to the house. The larger trucks couldn't make it back to the house.

The house had almost burned down before we arrived. The house's utilities were fed by gas. The fire had burned the gas line in half. The free flowing gas only fed the flames. Crews were unable to save anything. It was a total loss.

My response area included the airport. I responded to many calls for airport assists for planes landing under distress.

The area under my responsibility had a high-rise district. There were separate access elevators and towers, depending on where you wanted to go. Residents had storage units that were only accessible from the parking garages.

Many businesses and restaurants occupied the lower floors. Fire alarms were dispatched frequently in these buildings. One particular fire alarm turned out to be a real fire upon our arrival. The scene was managed with limited crews, but the fire was put out quickly.

There were some large commercial structures that were unoccupied in my area. Some were subdivided and used as separate businesses. These smaller areas shared a common attic area and weren't divided.

There had been several fires in these smaller units. When there was a fire, the open box area filled with smoke and limited the visibility of crews to operate in. Crews had some close calls while fighting these fires. The most serious fire created a challenge for crews because it was a deep-seated fire in the center of the building. The fire was challenging to reach to extinguish but controlled enough to limit its spread. This made the fire difficult to locate.

Ultimately the building was condemned, and homeless people took up residence. The final fire resulted in the building's collapse. Fire was visible through the roof, and the fire's location was evident. There was no benefit to fight the fire inside as the risks outweighed any benefit.

There were many residential fire responses as well. My response area had a high potential for fires. I was running the majority of them. Three other chiefs worked in other areas of the city each shift. One of the chiefs who bordered my response area would respond to my cases. He tried to arrive on scene first and take command of the fires in my area. He was well liked by senior officers. He was one of their friends from the FEMA team. He intimidated people. I was not deterred and continued to respond to my calls. He didn't respect my authority in my own battalion. I copied his tactic and started responding to calls in his battalion. It became a competition of who could arrive on scene first.

On large fires, the second chief can move forward. If a fire isn't that large and the next chief moves forward, they can essentially take command away from the incident commander. A majority of the time, I arrived first on the scene to calls in my area. On one of the occasions he arrived first, I moved forward and took command back. It was unprofessional but a game essential to maintaining control of my battalion.

He didn't like the fact that he was losing. Our game ended after I successfully moved forward and took control of one of his fires. Notorious for doing so, one of his crews had neglected to lay a supply line in to an obvious fire. They emulated his bad example and only wanted to beat everyone to the fire. They wanted to go interior and leave the water supply for someone else. He had to call units out of the structure until a water source could be secured.

You have to have water to put out a fire. Securing a water supply is the most important function performed on a scene. Most of the fire was on the rear of the townhouses. A ladder truck in my battalion had been assigned to the call and had secured a water source because a supply line had not been established. They were able to pull a hand line off their truck and extinguished the fire.

Fire attack is not a normal function for a ladder truck. They have many other tasks to complete. It was done that day because they had the only water supply. The normal functions of the ladder were completed. The heavy rescue squad was on the rear of the structure and assisted the ladder truck in utility control and ladder placement. They were able to back up the ladder.

The new strategy was communicated to this chief. The crews were able to complete a search and extinguish the fire before the engine on the front ever secured a water source.

After the fire was out and the searches were completed, I gave the fire-under-control status. Then I gave him back control of operating crews and cleared the scene. There wasn't anything left to complete but overhaul. He was frustrated and angry about the circumstances but couldn't argue about the outcome. Extensive fire loss was prevented, and the incident was controlled more quickly.

It was not turning out to be in his best interest to continue the competition because he was losing. He only looked foolish in the process.

Later I would have a multifamily, well-involved fire that had progressed to several units and gotten in the attic. He didn't respond. The fire chief didn't respond either. The competition only made me perform at a higher level. The challenge to not leave them anything to do when they arrived was my motivation.

I became better in fire command and control of fires by utilizing this strategy and didn't require assistance.

Holidays would still bring out senior-staff response to fires. The newly promoted deputy chief responded to a second-alarm fire in my area. He had a reputation for yelling and not having proper scene discipline. He was out of control on a fire years prior while at the technical-rescue station. I was working a trade on his shift and driving for him.

Upon arrival at the multifamily residential structure, the only thing on fire was the woman who resided in the residence. Her boyfriend had poured a flammable liquid on her and then lit her on fire. In her attempt to get away from him, she had set small spot fires on her way out of the house.

She was overcome by flames and perished on the sidewalk outside. The scene was horrific. All that remained were her charred remains. The truck wouldn't go in pump. The manual override was used without success. The engine behind mine was used to supply a hand line.

The fire victim was smoldering and obviously already dead when crews arrived. With the delay in water, the captain at the time but now a newly promoted deputy chief proceeded to yell and scream at everyone on scene. Most of his screaming was directed at me because I was the driver and there was a delay in getting water to the hand line.

The truck had an electrical problem that prevented it from going into pump. The manual operation of engaging the pump required two people because it had to be bumped into gear at the same time the valve on the pump panel was engaged. It was not something that could be accomplished alone. Weekly checks were conducted, but during maintenance, two people performed the function.

Firefighters are in the most control of the incident. Their emotions shouldn't be part of an already unfortunate situation. Discipline has to be maintained no matter how dire conditions appear. Focus should be on the goal you are trying to accomplish.

He was so theatrical on this multifamily residential fire that it couldn't be missed. Crews later came up and gave me praise for keeping my focus during his outburst.

His lack of control only gave me more resolve to remain calm. My focus was the command and control of the incident. He wasn't helpful, but I wasn't accustomed to receiving help. These experiences were helpful in future calls. Each experience helped me become better prepared for the next call for service.

Bigger and more challenging personnel issues were on the way.

CHAPTER TEN

360 Walk Around

Every few years, the battalion chiefs were transferred. It was my turn to take a position in administrative services. I was proficient in fire operations, but there was an opportunity to transfer into a position as the chief of training.

It was an influential position. There had never been a female chief of training. The training center was a regional training facility used by several surrounding cities. Our city was a large metro department, and the training center had its own budget. There was some resistance to me getting the position, but the district chief over the training division was the prior captain from the technical-rescue station. I had given him technical expertise on the technical-search component.

I had worked hard for him there, so he knew I would work and function at a high level. When he was my captain, he would frequently go to his bunkroom and sleep and watch television during the day while the station work and reports were completed. My job included completing all the fire reports and a majority of his administrative work. He had a saying that he repeated about an hour into every twenty-four-hour shift. The saying was "end of work day," or EOWD for short. When he got promoted to chief, the shift got him a new helmet shield that had EOWD on it.

Staffing for my shift was an auxiliary function when I worked in fire operations. That included making sure there were enough people on each truck to meet the minimum staffing for the truck. The trucks had to have people with the right qualifications. Each truck needed someone qualified to drive. Not everyone knew how to operate a ladder truck or tanker. The rescue squads that handled hazmat and technical rescue required personnel with special training. Some trucks required a paramedic. The cab of each truck needed an officer or someone qualified to work in the capacity as the officer if he or she was off. Each truck had criteria to meet to be considered fully staffed.

A primary search of the roster included filling immediate needs to fill short-staffed trucks. This would give me an overall idea of how vacancies needed to be filled for the day. The secondary search identified the special needs the person on relief might have required.

A size-up of the roster would identify what vacancies needed to be filled first. Specific requirements were the hardest to fill. It might require the callback of an officer, a paramedic, a driver of a ladder or tanker, or the person might require special training to be on one of the squads or in the marine division. Sometimes the needs were greatest for crews further away, and the relief was taken care of first because it was going to take longer to relieve crews trying to get off duty.

Each morning firefighters would call in if they were sick and unable to show up for their shift. Each station would list a name that was available for relief if they had more than the minimum staffing required. I was the gatekeeper to grant leave for the whole shift to ensure the minimum number of people were working.

To make the staffing easier to manage the department used an electronic staffing program. This was my project. Each battalion chief was assigned a project to manage the many different activities needed to keep a fire department running on top of their normal emergency operations duties. My responsibilities included managing this program and the marine division and running emergency calls.

Some projects were more time consuming and demanding than others. Some battalion chiefs were busier than others.

My supervisor at the technical-rescue station and while at training had oversight of this electronic staffing tool. He had me manage the whole project. He surrounded himself with the hardest working employees. His division operated at a highly efficient level. This put him in a good position to become promoted to the next level. He arranged to have me work in whatever division he was assigned to. He received the credit, but I was gaining experience. This gave me opportunities to work at the next level. This is why he now wanted me as the battalion chief of training because he knew from experience I was a hard worker.

As expected I worked at a high level of proficiency. There were many responsibilities to operate a regional training facility. Although a demanding position, I had many positive experiences working at the training center. Products of my time there included the tactics of positive-pressure attack (PPA) and vent-enter search (VES). As a result of the training, crews made a successful rescue of a trapped fire victim utilizing VES. The call would go on to be the state's call of the year. The PPA training attracted so much interest that other jurisdictions asked to attend the training.

My job included researching and planning future training events for our department. I formed relationships with the military while at fire training. My position required me to sit on a committee with surrounding training chiefs from other fire departments. As a result of the contacts I made, I was able to schedule an aircraft-crash-simulator training session with the military. The threat of a plane crash existed because of the many military bases in our area. We had not had one, and the odds of it happening were overdue. The training was scheduled a year and a half out. As soon as the whole department made it through the training, the city experienced a military jet crash.

Three fire academies were completed during my time as the chief of training. Two of the academies were held at the same time, something the department had never attempted before. There were many vacancies; more people were hired to attend an academy than there were spots for them to attend.

Because of the vacancies in fire operations, no field training instructors (FTIs) were provided during these simultaneous academies. Other academies had received the extra staff. Confidence existed in my ability to produce results regardless of logistical support. A fire recruit academy is an extensive eight-month academy. It takes many instructors to conduct live burns and some of the other dangerous training evolutions that are conducted in a fire academy.

The first shift day or twenty-four-hour shift was conducted during the dual academies. The concept was so well received that it was presented at a national training-instructor conference. The high demands of three company in-service (CIS), two ladder in-service (LIS), two officer in-service (OIS), annual career path classes required for promotion, National Fire

Academy (NFA) classes, and many video shop projects including a monthly video program were maintained. Special-operations classes were provided for the squads, and an annual national technical-rescue collapse school was held.

Since the training center was a regional facility, it was used by the surrounding jurisdictions. The burn building was used on nights and weekends to accommodate the heavy demand on the structure. Other fire departments used the building, and it was used for the two recruit academies. To accommodate the demand, the training facility was open seven days a week, sometimes until late at night.

The staff at the training center was a highly qualified and motivated group of individuals some of the best in the nation. They presented material for several new fire tactics and were asked to present them at a national training-instructor conference. They worked hard and were dedicated. A lot was expected of them, and they were held to a high standard.

There were many administrative functions as the training chief. The position normally wouldn't involve more than maintaining command of live burns.

The staff was working at a high level for a long time with no relief, so I put myself in the rotation for these burns. Some of these burns were conducted in the summer, along with evolutions in a flashover chamber that experienced high heat. The toll of the heat was exhausting for instructors. It was such a physical demand that one of the instructors had to be transported to the hospital and an IV started because he was dehydrated and experiencing severe muscle cramps.

The instructors had to teach fire recruits in the morning, so I stayed to lock the facility so they could leave and prepare for the morning classes at night after night burns. Rest was needed so they could continue to perform. It helped relieve some of their stress so they could continue to instruct during the day. My taking turns going inside the burn building was not understood by senior staff.

It was reaffirmed to me when there was a near-miss incident in the burn building at the training center. The incident took me back to my near-miss incident as a recruit. Crews were conducting live-fire burn evolutions. The scenario required crews to locate the fire and then knock down or darken the fire. They were to conduct a search, know when it was safe to ventilate, and check for fire extension.

Crews were directed to just knock the fire down, because if they put them out entirely, it was hard to restart the built burn boxes for the next fire evolution. The scenarios were the same for each crew making entry because the scenario was testing specific skills. The elements were basic fire tactics, but it was a requirement to participate in one live-fire burn a year. If crews don't encounter a fire during the year because they are assigned to a station with low call volume, these training fires helped keep them proficient in fire attack.

The instructors had prebuilt a box of hay and wood pallets to use for fire evolutions. It was done to be able to start the next fire evolution sooner. Visibility was limited after the first burn due to smoke still being present in the building. Usually the box wasn't built until after the prior fire evolution was conducted. It added to the fire load and combustibles in the burn building. Only one box was built so the burn could be controlled. It was a night burn because the recruit academy was held during the day. The instructors were exhausted from the night and day instruction. Mistakes were made when crews were fatigued.

Boxes of hay and straw were only placed where you planned to burn. The materials were highly flammable. The crew participating in the scenario located the fire and knocked it down as directed. They conducted a search and then asked for the fan to be started to initiate ventilation. The ladder operator asked his crew if they were sure they wanted the fan started. The officer of the crew confirmed he wanted ventilation started.

The ladder driver could hear the popping sound of burning materials and saw a glimmer of flame through the crack of the window when he placed the fan at the door. That is why he challenged the officer about being ready for ventilation.

He got confirmation to start the fan, so he did. The interior crew had moved on to their next task of checking for extension. This required that they use a ladder to access a metal attic scuttle to the third floor of the burn building. The access point was metal to withstand the multiple fires held in the building.

The fan was started when the crew was in the attic scuttle. An ember from the last fire was blown down the hallway. This ember ignited the box that had been prebuilt by the fire instructors down the hall.

There was an instructor called a safety on each floor with operating crews. The safety for that floor was with the crew at the attic scuttle. The box that caught on fire wasn't immediately noticed.

Heat rises. When the fan was started, it fanned the flames and increased the fire's involvement. The heat from this fire was being pushed up at this crew. The fire was detected by someone outside when the metal hinged window was blown open by the fan.

When a fire gets hot, the best place to be is near the floor. Part of the crew was either on the way up the ladder or in the scuttle opening. No one in the crew reported experiencing high heat or tried to move down to the floor.

They were resistant to move to the floor. Crews were familiar with the building because it was a concrete structure, and the floor plans rarely changed. They were resistant to revert to basic fire-attack methods.

No one was willing to admit it was hot or initiated any plan to evacuate. The gear firefighters wore kept them insulated and protected them from heat, but the heat intensified and created enough heat to melt their helmets. One person received facial burns where his flash hood had not covered his face.

After this incident, my rotations in the fire evolutions increased to help prevent fatigue in the instructors. This gave them an opportunity to take a break and sit one fire evolution out. I received criticism from the senior staff for doing so. They felt like it was beneath my position. My job is to provide incident command, but being able to physically fight fire is still a requirement for continued employment. Another battalion chief attended these live-fire burns and was able to take over the command role.

The battalion chief that competed with me for calls frequently came to participate in these live burns. He was praised for going inside on these same training fires. It didn't make sense to me, because it was all right for him but not for me, and I was the training chief. The message sent wasn't consistent.

During this busy time, there were still personnel issues to manage. It started out as a nuisance but would escalate to affect other functions of the training division. The administrative assistant was incapable of doing her job. This impeded the paperwork that was required to be completed that affected operations at the training facility. She was the wife of the deputy chief who had problems controlling his emotions on fire scenes, so it presented an unusual problem.

She refused to do her job, unwilling to complete basic functions required of her position. Others in the training division were performing her job. The tasks weren't hard, but the tasks were not their responsibility. The instructors were busy teaching classes. Paperwork she completed was returned from the state because it needed to be corrected.

Part of her job responsibilities included maintaining the electronic program that was used to schedule training at the training center. She wasn't proficient in maintaining the program. Scheduling battalion chiefs used the electronic program to schedule training for operational crews. She routinely got dates wrong. This resulted in both the instructors and training rooms becoming double booked. She consistently offered training on holidays and weekends when instructional staff was not working.

Part of my responsibility was to project training needs a couple of years in advance. Her frequent scheduling mistakes caused whole bookings for shifts to have to be rescheduled.

Fortunately, my experience managing the staffing program in operations prepared me to manage this program. It required that her work be routinely checked for accuracy. The regular checking for mistakes was time consuming. Any performance plans given to improve her job were reversed by senior staff as a personal favor.

Her job was mundane and didn't require special skills to perform, but it was critical for the smooth scheduling of training. She had been in her position for a long time, and there was no reason she shouldn't be able to perform the job correctly.

There were many classes held in the facility. It was imperative that the electronic scheduler was maintained to keep all the classes straight. My experience maintaining the staffing scheduler gave me the knowledge to override her errors.

She was the only one with administrator rights to make changes prior to my transfer there. My rights allowed me to make changes even though it wasn't my job to perform. She wasn't doing the basic functions of her job, whether by choice or because she was incapable. The chiefs' office didn't allow me to enforce her to perform her basic job functions.

Part of the demand on the training facility classes included bookings by the EMS division holding emergency medical technician (EMT) classes at the training facility on nights and weekends because most of their members were EMS volunteers and had regular employment during the day. Most of their classes were held on the off schedule the fire department held their classes. EMT classes for recruits were taught by the fire department.

Recertification classes were held for paramedics. Both fire and EMS paramedics were required to attend. Both the fire and EMS departments taught some classes. The course number and approval of classes were provided by EMS. The fire department had established a working relationship with EMS, so we were allowed to teach most of our own classes.

This use of training rooms in the facility for EMS classes added to the scheduling challenges. Someone had to stay on top of the scheduling program to ensure all required training was maintained. My identification of her frequent mistakes resulted in her developing a bad attitude.

I praised her when she accomplished something without making a mistake. I took her out for lunch and recognized her on administrative assistant day. I gave her gift cards to places she shopped, but my positive reinforcement didn't have any effect on her performance.

I documented her poor performance in her annual evaluation. She had never received a bad performance evaluation. No training chief prior to my arrival had dared do it. I documented facts of her performance in her evaluation that she couldn't grieve. I did it to try and get her to improve her performance. Her performance was fairly documented. My effort to get her to improve her performance was rewarded with retaliation.

The performance evaluation did not have the desired result. She came up with new ways to avoid performing her job. She complained of illness and psychiatric problems. Managing her was taking up unnecessary time. I provided her job improvement plans. She manipulated her position as the deputy chief's wife to avoid working. It wasn't fair to others. She wasn't required to perform her job, and my attempts to correct her behavior weren't supported by the fire chiefs' office.

She was the voice of the training center when someone called to enroll in a class. She booked classes for civilians and people outside our department. A lot of people she came in contact with had unpleasant experiences.

Because she had proven incompetent, another administrative assistant was asked to help with the upcoming recruit academy. The help was granted based on her documented failures in the past, one of which was to provide a graduation certificate for all the firefighters graduating in the prior recruit academy graduation, which was a requirement and basic function of her job.

She ordered the wrong book for the recruits to use in the upcoming academy. She ordered an out-of-date edition. When she reordered the correct book, she didn't order enough books

When I requested the assistance of another administrative assistant to help with the upcoming recruit graduation, she took offense. The graduation was going to be held in a large venue. She requested an open door with the fire chief about it. She didn't want the other administrative assistant to help. She took it as a reflection of her inability to put one together, which it was.

She called the other administrative assistant and told her not to come.

She didn't have authority to make that decision. The other administrative assistant was needed. She made a mistake on the graduation programs. She hadn't had me proof it first. She made five hundred copies of a program that needed to be reprinted at a print shop. That was an unnecessary additional cost to the department.

She told me that if the other administrative assistant came to the graduation she wasn't coming. She didn't have authority to make that decision either. I required her to bring a doctor's note if she failed to come to the ceremony.

She had confidence that she could do anything she wanted to do since no one had supervised her and made her do her job before. She also had the fire chiefs' office support. Prior supervisors hadn't managed her in the past.

On the night of the graduation, she told me she had ripped her pants and needed to go home. No tear was visible, but she was given duties behind the stage so she wouldn't suffer any embarrassment. The embarrassment could have been that she would be seen there. She'd told everyone she wasn't coming.

A couple days after the graduation, she told me she had slipped down a couple of steps in the auditorium the night the graduation was held and hurt her back. She didn't make the notification until two days later. Department policy requires that you report any injuries right away. She didn't come to work the next day.

She called out sick. The injury was identified because she didn't have any remaining sick-leave balance to cover her absence. She was a thirty-year employee but took her sick and annual leave as soon as she earned it each month. There wasn't enough sick leave to cover being out of work for the day. When she was contacted to let her know she would be on out on leave without pay, she told me about her injury.

Her low-leave balances were a common occurrence. Department policy requires fire chiefs' approval before you can be on leave without pay. The required paperwork was filled out to report her injury and forwarded to the safety division. Her injury was denied. She had been walking at the time of the accident. Workman's compensation denied the claim based on walking not being a special job skill required for her position. Workmen's compensation claims are paid as a result of becoming injured while performing a special skill required for your job. After she was told her claim was denied, she immediately felt better and came to work.

Her job required her to send out emails to notify the entire department about upcoming training. Her emails were unprofessional and threatening. She was counseled about the use of the city's email system and warned that future occurrences would result in discipline. Her use of the email system didn't improve and broke city policy. She received discipline, but it was reversed by the fire chiefs' office.

This took away my ability to enforce her proper use of the email system. She continued the abuse of policy, and that's when she participated in an email exchange about the fire department's hiring process.

Any discipline to correct her job performance was circumvented by the fire chiefs' office. If I wrote her any discipline, they overturned it. She engaged in nasty emails about the departments hiring process that ultimately ended up on the local news. It was embarrassing to the entire department because it was a negative news story about the hiring process in our department.

That email became part of a news story run about the department's hiring process. She was upset because her son did not meet the minimum qualifications to be eligible to participate in our department's hiring process. She personally attacked the HR manager from our department. She attacked them for her son's inability to receive an interview. She knew if he got an interview he would be hired because of who he was.

The chiefs' office wanted me to discipline her. Fortunately, the news story didn't connect her relationship with our deputy chief, but the email was still embarrassing to the department. I told my chief that I couldn't administer the discipline but that someone at a higher level had to do it, because they had taken away my effectiveness to discipline her. If the discipline was received from me, it wouldn't mean anything to her.

He assured me they would administer the discipline because it was a serious offense. The department experienced severe embarrassment because of the incident. She was a member of the department and hadn't supported the hiring process. Others that had engaged in the same group email were receiving discipline. The hiring process wasn't flawed; it just didn't produce the outcome she wanted.

She never received any discipline.

When transferred into the training division, the chief who I replaced told me the worst thing about working there would be managing this administrative assistant. He was right. The training division was great. Many worthwhile training projects occurred during my time there. It was satisfying to train the next generation of firefighters and keep up with new training in the field. Managing her would be the challenge of the division.

He hadn't dared discipline her because it was political suicide. He and the prior two training chiefs were all promoted to the next rank. The training division provided many opportunities for growth and development in the department. None of them had attempted to discipline the deputy chief's wife or require she perform her job.

Managing her was still part of the job. She was out of control. I didn't do a good size-up. My strategy was ineffective. I didn't have the proper resources to attack this out-of-control fire. My chain of command expected a strong incident commander but didn't support my strategy.

My position in training required close communication with the chief's office. This provided access to confidential information that was only known by few. It gave me perspective on how the chief and his staff managed. It gave me a window into their management philosophy. It was revealing but disappointing.

Some of their practices were illegal and immoral. My hopes were to become promoted to change that. My assessment of fire conditions was inaccurate. They were satisfied with their strategy and tactics and weren't open to changing the way they attacked the fire.

I had inaccurately judged my ability to become promoted. Promotions weren't granted on education, skill, experience, or accomplishments. They weren't based on your ability to do the job or based on whether you were the best fit for a position. They were based on whether the fire chief liked you and what you were willing to do.

I was not willing to conform to the requirements to become promoted. The management philosophy went against what I considered ethical and would compromise my integrity. My refusal to comply with their expectations became another turning point. Promotion wasn't a possibility. Selections were based on compliance to expectations and relationships formed with the chief.

The small correct choices along my career made the decision to maintain my integrity easier, even though it would end the progression of my career. Those small choices helped me make bigger decisions later. A promotion wouldn't be a reward if it meant a sacrifice of my personal integrity.

During the fire academy, some recruits couldn't maintain the minimum qualifications to continue in the fire academy. Firefighting isn't a good fit for everyone. Some couldn't meet the physical requirements to perform the job.

Several were claustrophobic and not able to keep the face piece on during structural firefighting. Others didn't meet the academic requirements. They couldn't perform the basic requirements of the job.

Several recruits suffered injuries during training. Sometimes these injuries prevented them from continuing in the academy. The missed instructional time resulted in missing too much of the academy to graduate. Some training was a prerequisite for future training. They didn't qualify to continue in the academy because the missed training was a requirement for graduation.

There was pressure to get the recruits out to fire operations. Fire operations were short staffed because of the many vacancies that existed. The lack of adequate personnel to run an academy added to the challenge to try to catch recruits up that were behind.

The minimum number of days was provided to complete the fire academy. The requirements of the state had to be met. Our fire academy exceeded the expectations outlined by the state, but there still wasn't enough time to catch up the recruits who had missed an excessive amount of time in the academy. The schedule left no room for makeup time. There wasn't enough time to make up entire sections of training, even though it was attempted on nights and weekends.

The senior chiefs wanted me to falsify the training records to reflect that the recruits had fulfilled the state requirement. Laws regulate the training and certification of firefighters. A department can be found negligent for failing to train firefighters properly. This was simply something I wouldn't do. I took the responsibility of firefighting training seriously. No recruit was allowed to graduate from the academy unless they were qualified.

This was a large fire to control, the integrity of the training delivered and personnel issues with the administrative assistant needed to be maintained. My size-up required the strategy of a direct offensive attack, although this was dangerous. I didn't think a defensive attack would be effective.

The pressure to follow the wishes of senior staff went against my personal integrity and threatened exposures. Despite the offensive fire attack, the fire would extend and affect my ability to become promoted any further. To protect exposures, the offensive strategy I utilized included involving the state to validate the inability to graduate recruits who weren't qualified. I sent an email to the state, genuinely asking if there wasn't some sort of exception that we could use not to have hazmat training completed before the end of the academy and copied my chain of command so they knew I had sent it. I knew what the state's answer would be, and it also let the state know that we had some recruits that had not received all the required state training. This tactic supported the strategy to maintain my personal integrity.

My refusal to comply with the wishes of senior staff in part resulted in being transferred after the academy was over. The deputy chief's wife didn't like me, and I wouldn't conform to the chiefs' wishes to falsify records. Part of the punishment for these offenses would be a transfer to a slow battalion. This was the common pattern of punishment if you disobeyed the chief.

The result of trying to manage her was that I was retaliated against for doing my job. My transfer back in fire operations meant her husband would be my supervisor. This experience was the first time I considered the fire being fought was outside my control to extinguish.

Right after the recruit graduation, notice of my transfer was given. The reason given, however, was that the chief was embarrassed because the graduation wasn't called a *regional* fire academy. That one word, *regional*, that was omitted had supposedly embarrassed the chief. The omission of the term *regional* had been dropped for over twenty years in our department. The minimum qualifications are met by the state, but a true regional academy would include recruits from other jurisdictions in the same fire academy. Our city had not had a regional fire academy in over twenty years.

The fire chief sits on a regional chiefs' committee. My regional training committee was a subcommittee of the fire chief's committee. One of the tasks of the training committee was to come up with the criteria of a fire academy that all cities could follow. The state outlines the requirements for the minimum training hours to certify firefighters. Each city adds additional training requirements based on the needs of the jurisdiction.

Some cities only used the state criteria, while our city only used the state requirements as a minimum requirement baseline, far exceeding the requirements of the state. The feasibility of what should be included in a regional academy couldn't be agreed upon by all jurisdictions.

Each jurisdiction had unique challenges to its region that require special training to prepare its firefighters. Everyone agreed the minimum state requirements should be met but couldn't agree that state requirements were enough and what other training should be included in an academy.

The policies of each city were different for discipline, physical fitness, and appearance. The state only required a score of 70 percent to pass a written test, while our city required 80 percent as the passing rate. Not all cities had a requirement for a higher test score. These and other differences prevented establishing one regional requirement for recruit firefighters.

The chief's group was currently trying to evaluate if a regional academy was possible. This would mean that if a firefighter received his or her training in another city and transferred employment to a different city, the firefighter wouldn't have to go through another fire academy. Our chief required all new hires to go through our fire academy because our city exceeded the minimum requirements of the state.

To say the fire chief was embarrassed by the omission of the word *regional* during our city's recruit graduation was trivial. Saying the word *regional* didn't follow his original direction, which had been clear to me. He was never going to agree to a regional fire academy unless it was the same as our current academy or exceeded our already higher standard of training.

The task given by the training committee to standardize a regional training academy was an exercise not expected to be able to be accomplished. The regional chiefs' committee was entertaining the idea to remain politically agreeable. Few of the fire chiefs had any intention of changing the existing requirements in their fire academies. Some of the fire departments in the region did attend each other's fire academies because they only hired a few firefighters at a time, and it was more cost effective.

The challenges of these academies were that the requirements for their recruits were different. It was hard to manage these regional academies with different rules for different fire recruits. Our city only held academies when there were enough vacancies to fill a whole academy.

To hear him say that omitting the word *regional* was confusing to me and didn't make sense. The omission had started many years ago, by prior chiefs of training who were now complaining about it.

Our department provided space for other fire academies, but they did not participate in our city's fire academy. Our facility had the burn building, which was the only one available for some jurisdictions. Our city did not have spots to allow other cities to fill any positions in one of our fire academies.

Our video department was exceptional. They provided teleprompters for the speakers to utilize in the upcoming recruit graduation. My speech was prepared and rehearsed, and I used the teleprompters, making my delivery smooth and polished. I asked the commander of the military base that had recently suffered a large jet crash to be the keynote speaker. His speech was well prepared, and both of our presentations went well.

The fire chief had not prepared his speech and chose not to use the teleprompters. His presentation looked unpolished, and he looked ill prepared. If there was any embarrassment at the recruit graduation, it was because of the stark difference of others' presentations.

During this time frame, I participated in a promotional process. There was little hope that it would result in a promotion because of the events going on at the time. The chief's normal routine was to preselect who he was going to promote anyway. The selections became apparent before promotional processes would begin. In most cases, they were his personal friends whose association was developed while he had been a captain at the technical-rescue station.

To confirm my feelings about the chance of a promotion, my value to senior staff became evident. I had been having problems with the EMS division releasing our fire medics. Their medical director signed off and released all medics whether their department taught the class or not.

The chief over EMS had a history of lying. The fire recruits were required to ride on ambulances after they had passed their written test. They had to ride with an EMS medic to get their skills sheets signed off, but the EMS departments medics were busy and sometimes had conflicts because they were trying to release some of their own medics as well.

Even with these conflicts, they wouldn't relinquish the authority to sign off the skills for fire paramedics. There had been several prior conversations with this EMS chief about our fire medics ride schedule with his releasing medics. Both parties had agreed to a schedule, which was tight. Overtime was being incurred in operations until these fire recruits were released. Their ride time would occur over a holiday.

If their ride time wasn't completed, it would conflict with the second recruit academy's ride time. The ride time had to be completed before they could sit to take the EMS state test that was already scheduled for a certain day. Senior staff's time frame didn't allow for anything to go off schedule.

When it was time for their ride time, the EMS chief said they needed to take a class before they could ride. He had never mentioned this class requirement, and verification was made before the ride time that they had met all the requirements of his department to ride. After research and my challenging him, it was determined that our fire medics didn't need to take the class he was referring to.

His next tactic was to say he was pulling their ride time because some paperwork wasn't filled out they should have completed during class. The paperwork he was referring to was something they required their volunteers to sign that had to do with reimbursement for the cost of the training if someone didn't fulfill their commitment to volunteer. The paperwork wasn't relevant to fire recruits because they were not volunteering with their department. The EMS department had not paid for or taught their training.

When that obstacle was overcome, he changed the reason that the fire recruits couldn't ride because an EMS provider reported that one of the fire recruits had been disrespectful during his or her ride time. When the incident was investigated, no one could be found that would make a complaint or knew about the occurrence. He was asked on multiple occasions what was required for the fire recruits to ride, but he wasn't forthcoming with the information and changed the rules along the way.

Ultimately, the chain of command got involved from both departments. The political climate between the two departments was strained before the academy. It was increasing hard to work with him since he wasn't being cooperative or truthful. The chain of command had to become involved because his latest excuse was going to upset the schedule and affect the start date they could begin their work shifts in fire operations.

The EMS chief avoided talking to me. We held the same rank in our departments. His office was in our building. He had been sending emails up my chain of command about the ride schedule. Unfortunately, they were responding, and their responses gave him an excuse to avoid working with me.

I made a request for them to stop responding to his emails. They are micromanagers, so they lacked the capacity to do so. This EMS chief became involved in the medics' schedule. My chain of command was becoming involved with it, too. This was a task normally completed by a medic on the EMS side and an instructor on the fire side. This task was far beneath the chiefs' ranks.

An emergency meeting was scheduled over the holidays to work out our departments' conflicts. My female captain over EMS training, my deputy chief, and this EMS chief were in attendance. The fire deputy chief requested the battalion chief over fire medics in operations attend the meeting. His assigned program was the release of fire medics to fire operations. He was the battalion chief I competed for calls with and was the fire chief's next pick for promotion.

The fire deputy chief referred to me and the female fire captain by our first names but called the other two in the room by their rank. The EMS chief became so comfortable because of this omission that he admitted he had a problem working out the schedule because he didn't have anyone to talk to about it. That wasn't true because we had already worked out a schedule for the fire recruits to ride. He was just changing the agreement.

I told my deputy chief ahead of the meeting that part of the reason we had a problem with the schedule was because the EMS chief refused to communicate with me on the ride schedule. The EMS chief's lack of acknowledgment of my authority was part of the problem identified as not being able to work out a ride schedule. I had explained to my deputy chief that his response to the ride schedule emails was further impeding efforts to attain a schedule.

He was reminded that the ride schedule had already been completed by a medic and an instructor. The problem was the EMS chief had become involved and pulled the agreed-upon ride schedule. Our deputy chief was asked to stop responding to his emails to avoid duplicate confusing directions that prevented the ride schedule to move on as planned.

When the EMS chief made this admission of not having anyone to talk to, I expected my deputy chief to correct him. It was a communicated factor identified in why there was a problem with our communication. My deputy chief didn't respond. This required a direct strategy. I corrected him and reminded him that I was his contact.

At the conclusion of the meeting, nothing was remedied, and the goal of getting a commitment for a ride schedule for the fire recruits was not agreed upon. It was frustrating because the meeting had been called to work out the problems with the ride schedule, but one had not been agreed to.

The deputy chief had not accomplished the goal the meeting was called for. Little was accomplished, except a growing realization that the possibility of a promotion was something that could never be achieved.

The only thing apparent was the obvious disrespect of my authority and value within the department. The goal to obtain fire medics ride time was ultimately reached. The EMS chief went on to be involved in an administrative hearing resulting from his unprofessional behavior and record of lying and falsifying training records.

My strategy of working hard, acquiring higher education, and diversifying my knowledge of different fire department divisions was backfiring. My strategy to achieve acceptance as a chief in the fire department was not effective. The realization that the resources required to change those perceptions weren't available. It was a fire not able to be extinguished.

It was a shocking realization. My strategy of working hard and determination had produced results before, but this fire extended beyond my capacity to control. There weren't sufficient resources. There were no crews to help fight this type of fire. I had spent so much time offensively attacking the fire that I didn't realize that the fire had extended past the point of origin.

My determination and effort weren't enough to extinguish this type of fire. There were signs along the way, but they hadn't deterred me. Fires are challenging, but there had never been one that I couldn't extinguish.

The realization that the fire was outside my capacity to extinguish was devastating. Fires cause so much damage there had to be something that could be saved. Perhaps my efforts had made a difference for others that would follow me, but one of them witnessed my failure in that meeting.

This meeting occurred two days before my promotional process. This realization was made right before going into my interview. The deputy chief from the meeting was on the interview panel.

The other battalion chief in that meeting was the selected choice for the next promotion, but he failed to submit his paperwork to the city HR department in the advertised time frame. The fire chief went to the city human resource department and requested that he still be able to participate in the promotional process anyway since the battalion chief was the fire chief's selection, but HR denied his request because it was a basic requirement to participate in the process.

The fire chief then went to the city attorney's office to try to get it changed, and they denied his requests. When the fire chief couldn't get his selection included in the process, other participants realized the opportunity, and it gave us hope for a chance for promotion.

This battalion chief denied entry in the process would go on to make the promotion in the next process.

Knowing there was a chance helped to shake off the feelings experienced at the time. I focused on all the reasons I was qualified for the promotion. I had more education, certification, training, and tenure than the other candidates. I had been in many divisions within the department and was currently in an influential position within the department.

Later, it was disclosed by one of the senior chiefs who attended that weekly meeting that another person had already been chosen as a replacement in the next senior staff chief's weekly meeting. It was good no one knew because knowing this would have deflated the performances of everyone participating.

The replacement selected candidate was told to study a specific document and bring it into his interview. No other candidate was given any preknowledge about any of the promotional questions or allowed to bring any outside material into the interview. Candidates had to be a battalion chief for four years to participate in the process. Acting time was allowed to count toward meeting the requirement to allow some to participate where it hadn't been in the past.

The rules of the promotional process were that only those that had done well in the interview would be recommended to the fire chief for an interview for promotion. The person they had preselected to receive the promotion hadn't done well enough in the interview even with the benefit of knowing what questions would be asked and having material in the interview to assist him.

He wasn't in the group recommended by the interview panel to move forward for an interview with the chief, so the rules were changed to allow him to move forward anyway. Others who were recommended to move forward in the process didn't. The fire chief promoted who he wanted regardless of the promotional process outcome. The rest of us were just participants to make it appear like a fair process.

This newly promoted district chief came into my office soon after to ask for my assistance in an upcoming battalion chief process. He wanted to ensure a certain candidate made it through to the next phase in the process. That candidate's written score going in was low. As an assessor, he wanted me to grade him high because he wanted his friend promoted. Part of my responsibilities at the training center was to produce a tactical video for the fire problem for the promotional processes and sit as an assessor. He wanted to know details about the tactical problem, which was the next phase of the promotional process so he could share it with this preferred candidate to increase his chances of success. As an assessor for the oral part of the promotional process, he wanted me to score this candidate high no matter how he performed.

His request was absurd. There was no way I was going to fix scores in a promotional process. He became angry and confused because I wouldn't even consider it. He had no remorse for making the request. He said the fire chief had told him to do it, so he didn't see why it was wrong.

The individual they wanted to promote was another friend from the early days at the technical-rescue station. He never considered how ironic it was that he had been promoted using the same unfair practices. He gave me little respect or consideration that I was a victim of the way promotions were made. We had been in the same promotional process. He was confident. He never saw me as competition. He had been told he would receive the promotion and knew he would receive future promotions.

It was unfair and unethical. My personal experience in a promotional process made me especially critical that they remain fair and equitable. If a tactical problem seemed to present an unfair advantage to one of the participants, I directed the video department to change the whole tactical problem. It was designed to be generic so it didn't present an unfair advantage to anyone who might have run a similar case to the one presented in the tactical problem.

During this discussion he admitted he was told what the questions would be in his promotional process and had been told to bring the document into the interview to reference. He said the fire chief told him he would be promoted before the process started. A couple of the district chiefs confirmed this later and said that promotions were discussed in their senior-staff meetings prior to promotional processes.

He was so confident he shared the information. In his mind it was all right because the fire chief had asked him to do it.

I never said anything about his request because it wouldn't change anything and it would only be denied. He was angry I wouldn't comply with his request, so he went to complain to the city HR person running the upcoming battalion chiefs process. He had gone to high school with her. He admitted fire chief had already made his selection. He asked her what he could do to make sure this person did well in the process.

He was voicing his frustration that the list that was generated from her process hadn't produced the person they wanted to promote. She was shocked at his admission. He was confused by her response because he couldn't understand why it was wrong. The fire chief had asked him to do it, and he was willing to do whatever the chief wanted. This, of course, was another reason he had been the chief's selection for promotion.

The city HR person now had a duty to act. The admission was invalidating her promotional process. The HR director and the city attorney's office became involved. When the fire chief was asked if he had made the request, he denied it. What else could he do? Who would be so stupid as to freely talk about such an unethical practice?

Later when I was asked if he had requested my assistance in fixing scores in a promotional process, more similar requests were revealed. It was determined that he had asked other assessors to do the same thing. His only punishment was his inability to be an assessor in any future promotional processes. The ironic part is that he went on to be promoted to a level where he made the selections for promotions.

When asked why I didn't report it, I told them I had no intention of complying with the request and thought no one would believe me, and I knew he would deny making the request. It would just have looked as though I was disgruntled about being passed over for promotion.

Since the promotional process was under investigation, it was too risky to promote the person they'd originally wanted to. He had scored too low to make the promotion believable. That list was terminated so a new process could be run and allow this individual another chance to become promoted for another known vacancy. A new process was held just a few months later, and he was promoted off that list. The fire chief had a soft spot for individuals who didn't do well in promotional processes. He was promoted off a nonrecommended list himself. Later, the educational qualifications were changed to allow for smoother promotions without grievances.

My transfer was made as I predicted. It is customary that prior administrative chiefs get to request assignments because they have fulfilled their administrative requirements. My request was to two battalions with vacancies. I received neither transfer-request assignment. It became increasingly evident that my strategy should change to a defensive one. I was being transferred to a slow-running battalion, and my new supervisor had been the best man at the deputy chief's wedding to his wife, the administrative assistant at the training center.

More ethical dilemmas were encountered in my administrative position than in fire operations. The information that was available in my services position provided me with disappointing information. Suspicions were confirmed there. Promotions weren't based on merit but on who you knew. This stopped some of the best candidates from even participating. It was fruitless to try because everyone already knew who the fire chief was going to select.

There were pools predicting who was going to be promoted, and everyone was getting pretty good at guessing the next pick. They were identified by their presence on camping trips with the chief. In betting, these candidates would have been long shots because the candidates selected were oftentimes the least qualified.

CHAPTER ELEVEN

Protect Exposures

Some people may think nepotism in the workplace shouldn't be allowed, but there is a tradition of family in the fire service. My father-in-law was one of the first seven firefighters hired in the department in 1947 when the town became a city. He retired after thirty-eight years of service as the deputy chief of fire services. I married his middle son, who also served in the department for thirty-two years. My mother-in-law, along with some other firefighters' wives, started a ladies auxiliary group that responded to working fires and essentially performed the same duties our rehabilitation and salvage units perform today.

My husband attained his ranks earlier than I did because he had been in the department longer. Usually our work shifts were either on opposite shifts or one of us had an administrative position, while the other worked shift work. As a married couple at the same rank, work issues were approached neutrally. Neither one of us inappropriately talked about work issues. At times there was a difference of opinion, but our work life remained professional.

My father-in-law's brother, or our uncle, was in the department for thirty-seven years. He married a woman with grown children, and I supervised one of those children. I considered the potential for perceived preferential treatment because she was family to me.

I wanted to make sure it was appropriate for me to supervise her. She was married to a battalion chief in the department. It was possible to have family members in the same department if the relationships were kept professional. The fire service had a long tradition of generations of families in the fire service. It was a commendable tradition. Upon my retirement, it was the first time in forty-seven years that there hadn't been a Seagrave in the fire department.

The experience of supervising the deputy chief's wife at the training center turned out to be an example of how nepotism in the workplace didn't work out. Her behavior was unprofessional. The response to her job performance and behavior was an example of not being able to separate personal feelings from good departmental decisions.

Nepotism can lead to one being put in situations where choices have to be made between families and doing what is best for an organization. My father-in-law administered discipline to his brother during his career. It wasn't personal; it was business.

Shift change then was at six o'clock. Firefighters slept at the fire station the night they came on duty. They would wake up the next morning in the fire station. A large majority of calls are run at night. After one of these nights running a lot of calls, my uncle slept in past when he should have been up one morning. The time he'd slept in was past the time allowed in the policy. My father-in-law had given his brother a reprimand for sleeping in at the fire station, even though he had been up all night running calls the night before. My uncle never slept in again.

My husband was the recipient of some department discipline involving a transfer process. He was negotiating with his district chief about what transfers needed to be made. Another chief wanted a master firefighter working in one of his stations. If he granted the transfer, it would leave his station without a master firefighter.

A master firefighter is someone who has demonstrated by taking a written test and completing a skill book that he or she is ready to perform the temporary duties of a captain. That person gets checked off by his or her captain while the captain rides behind that person in the jump seat. It gives the firefighter an opportunity to run calls and allows him or her to manage the unit under the supervision of the captain. The candidate had to be a firefighter for six years and demonstrate a certain skill set before he or she is allowed to take on the responsibilities of the captain.

My experience was much different. My training was accomplished by trial and error. My experience came early and quickly. It is safer and ensures the success of individuals to conduct the release of master firefighters using the current method.

My husband had another individual at the station who was within a few months of meeting the time requirement to ride up front. The individual had completed his skills-check-off book and ridden in the cab under a captain's supervision. My husband had a discussion with his district chief about the situation. The other station desperately needed a master firefighter because they didn't have one. If the transfer was granted, the other remaining firefighter would become a master firefighter a short time later.

My husband and his district chief mutually made a decision to allow the transfer and allow the other firefighter to ride in the capacity of the captain as a master firefighter if required. The only qualification he lacked was time. The district chief agreed to allow the firefighter to ride in the front of the cab in the captain's absence because the firefighter had met all the other requirements.

After the transfer occurred, the captain called out sick. The firefighter rode in the cab as planned. There was still a vacancy created on the truck that that had to be filled with a person off duty on overtime, referred to as a *callback*. This callback was a master firefighter. He knew he was the only master firefighter working. He assumed he would be riding in the cab.

When this master firefighter went back to his own shift, he questioned why the firefighter had been allowed to ride in the cab. The battalion chief on the other shift was participating in a promotional process with my husband, trying to get promoted. He pursued an investigation into the not-yet-ready master firefighter through his chain of command. The district chief from his shift didn't know about the arrangement, and he initiated an administrative hearing to investigate.

In the administrative hearing, my husband admitted to allowing the firefighter to ride in the cab of the truck as the captain, having done so only with his district chief's approval. By the time the administrative hearing was concluded, the firefighter had fulfilled the time required to obtain his master firefighter rank. My husband's district chief denied giving his approval, and my husband subsequently received discipline.

My husband had never received any discipline in the thirty years prior to this incident. He had always been a valued productive employee.

District chiefs frequently made selective exceptions to policies, following the example of the fire chief, who allowed people who weren't qualified by policy to participate in promotional processes. Exceptions were made for the qualifications required to fill acting positions. Then the time spent in these acting positions was allowed to be counted toward time in a position to qualify to participate in promotional processes.

Because of the inconsistencies, it sent confusing messages about what policies were going to be enforced. Ironically, during my time as the training chief, I was assigned to review the skill requirements necessary to qualify a firefighter to become a master fighter. Part of the direction given was to lower the time requirement necessary for a firefighter to qualify to become a master firefighter. More emphasis was placed on whether the skills were mastered than on the time requirement.

My experience was that some employee's couldn't be disciplined because of who they were. You suffered retaliation if you did discipline them, even if the discipline was deserved.

How politics work in an organization can have more to do with how you conform to accepted practices than written policies. This was a critical decision that would affect my eligibility for promotion. If an employee with a discipline problem and poor performance wasn't documented, it would break policy. If the deputy chief's wife was disciplined and accurately evaluated, there would be negative consequences. It was the right thing for me to do as her supervisor, even though it affected my ability to become promoted.

Some traditions in the fire service are good. There is a brother- and sisterhood in the fire service. Nepotism in the fire service is all right if rules are followed to avoid favoritism. Rules should be consistent and fair, but rules aren't fair if they aren't administered consistently.

My first fire chief ran a very different fire department than the one that exists today. Through the years there have been many new and improved practices that increase firefighter safety. Some of the biggest differences I noticed have been instances that involve chief officers' personal integrity and moral decision making.

My experiences with the early chiefs were different than more recent experiences. Early in my career, driving on the relief truck, there was a report of a car fire in a new neighborhood. The street names weren't on a map yet, and the address was hard to find because of it, so the location was found by following the smoke. There were many calls received because of the large amount of smoke seen. The deputy chief of operations came to the call because he was nearby and heard all the reports.

I was in the process of hand pulling about six hundred feet of three-inch supply hose to a hydrant. The car on fire was that far away from the nearest hydrant. The five hundred gallons of water carried on the truck were depleted and going to run out soon. The car was still on fire, and a water source was needed. The car had burned so long, the welded seal of the gas tank melted. The gas tank dumped its remaining gasoline on the road, and it was running down the street burning.

The deputy chief asked what he could do to help. I told him to pull the rest of the hose to the hydrant, which was another two hundred feet away. I needed to go back and ensure the truck hadn't run out of water yet. He readily complied with my request, even though he was dressed in a white dress shirt and even though the task was beneath his rank.

Another example involved a close call while responding to a residential fire driving the ladder truck. The back gate of a military base that was normally locked was used to get to the address more quickly. I had never been through the area. As the truck approached a curve, the passenger in the cab stated there were some turns ahead. I slowed the truck down to about thirty-five miles per hour, but it wasn't slow enough. As the curve approached, the road disappeared in a one hundred and eighty degree turn. I hit the brakes and wheeled the truck around. It took great effort to keep the truck on the pavement of the road.

The momentum and weight of the truck quickly changing direction caused the passenger side wheels to leave the ground. My first thought was that the truck was going to roll over, since the truck was top heavy because of the ladder on top. The sides of the road were sand. I exerted a lot of effort to keep from driving the truck right into a sand dune. Somehow the remaining wheels stayed on the road.

Slowly the truck started to come back down, and the wheels that were off the road suspended in the air came back down on the road roughly. My next challenge was to maintain control of the truck as it started to fishtail from the heavy weight of the truck coming back down and causing the truck to bounce. I anticipated that a tire would burst due to the impact of the weight of the truck coming back down so roughly.

There was a sign coming up. The front of the truck cleared the sign, but the rear end of the truck was coming toward the sign because the truck was fishtailing. The same maneuvers were used to correct a skid on ice. The truck straightened back out and missed the sign. Control was regained, no tire was blown, and the truck remained on the road.

Everyone was shaken, but we still had to respond to the dispatched residential fire. On the way to the address, my thoughts turned to what the deputy chief was going to do when he found out about the near-miss accident. He frequently told employees who had disappointed him that he was going to fire them. He was passionate about the department's equipment. He took personal pride in the department's trucks, and damaging one could result in termination. There was fear in disappointing him.

He didn't fire me, and it was a relief no one was hurt or killed. The accident would have been more serious if the truck had rolled over—it could have been fatal. The deputy chief rejected firing me because of the lesson I learned. He was a chief worthy of respect. My current deputy chief lacked leadership abilities. He wasn't a leader. He was a manager.

My first fire chief responded to a report of a residential fire our crew was dispatched to. The call happened to be in our area, but our unit had been relocated to another station while they attended training, so our response took longer. The first fire unit arriving on scene reported that it was a working fire.

The fire itself was located in the middle of a row of townhouses located on a dead end court. The attack engine communicated that they did not have a connection to the hydrant and needed us to supply water to them. My plan was to stop at the court and let the crew off the truck while the supply line was dropped to make a connection to the attack truck. The hydrant was further down the street in the direction of travel our unit had responded in from. Stopping there would allow our crew to assist in fire attack and victim searches more quickly. Then the water connection could be secured.

As the truck approached the fire scene, the fire chief started waving for us to turn down the court. If his direction had been followed, no connection could have been made to the hydrant. There would have been no permanent water supply for the attack engine.

It was hard to disregard the fire chief's direction, but a water supply is essential to extinguish a fire. I made a quick decision to go for the water supply. Because of the last-minute decision, I had to punch the gas pedal to power away from the turn down the court.

Fire operations continued smoothly, with no lapse in the water supply. The fire chief was standing in the bay when the truck returned from the fire. Everyone thought he had come by to praise them for performing well on the fire scene. The fire had been quickly extinguished. No one knew I had disobeyed his orders. All the trucks were backed in the bays and turned off. Everyone congregated at the rear of the trucks to talk to the fire chief.

His sunglasses were on his face, one of the lenses missing. When the direction of the truck was changed, exhaust had blown road debris in his face. The quick change of direction of the truck had blown dust and gravel into his face and knocked the sunglasses off the top of his head, and the lens had been popped out. Realizing what had happened was comical to me, and I started laughing.

He had a stern look on his face. The other firefighters couldn't believe my reaction when they realized what had happened. The fire chief laughed about it with me, but when packing hose that looked to be slipping off the back of the truck, he pushed me up in the hose bed. He shoved me up hard on the butt.

Prior emergency scenes had taught me not to obey everything directed to do. It sounds like disobeying orders, but my experiences taught me to think for myself. Not all directions were good ones.

An example of blindly listening to someone else resulted in an accident that taught me to rely on my own judgment. It was on a call while operating the ladder truck. I was driving the front end of the tiller truck. It was something that took a while before the opportunity became available. When the truck was new, they didn't want a female operating it. It wasn't until every shift had an accident and had damaged it that the opportunity was given for me to drive it. The opportunity to make my own dent in the truck became available.

The incident occurred on a summer evening during the busy tourist season. The truck was driven from the cab and steered from the rear. My training started in the rear, consisting of the front driver turning as fast as he could without any turn signal or verbal notice. If I didn't hit any cars sitting on the side of the road and the rear of the truck stayed out of the ditch and the truck stayed in between the lines of the road, permission was given for me to drive and operate the truck.

There was a third-floor motel room on fire located off a five-lane highway. There was still a lot of vehicle and walking traffic, and access to the motel was limited. The motel had a small, L-shaped parking lot that was completely full. The parking lot was so tight that the whole sixty-three-foot truck wouldn't fit in the parking lot.

The rear of the vehicle remained on the incline of the driveway into the parking lot and stuck out into one of the lanes of traffic. It was apparent that the motel's external standpipe system valves had been turned on in the stairways. When the system was supplied with water, it starting pumping water out in all the stairways, and the water was running down the stairways like a waterfall.

My ladder pipe would have to be used externally as the water supply. Crews had climbed to the third floor and needed my water supply to start fire attack. I pulled the ladder truck's bumper up as close as I could to the car parked in front of it.

I started the process of locking the cab stabilizing pins and putting the stabilizing outriggers out. This had to be completed before the ladder could be extended to the third floor.

When the truck representative delivered the truck, he said the lockdown pins locked the cab in place. This was accomplished by the pins making contact with the pad between the cab of the truck and the ladder section. The controls to place the outriggers out were on the ladder section. There was a level to the left of the controls to ensure the truck was level before the ladder was lifted out of the bed.

The outriggers themselves were between the controls and the cab of the truck. While trying to get the truck level, the weight was taken off the front tires enough that the cab starting to swing around. The lockdown pins had not done their job.

The department had requested an additional ten feet of ladder, which made the truck heavier. The truck was housed in an old building. The department had requested that the cab be shortened so the truck would fit in the old station.

These alterations didn't allow the lockdown pins to work as designed. I was ordered to push the outriggers all the way down and lift the whole truck up off the ground by the master firefighter in the cab of the truck. Some ladder trucks were designed to be operated this way.

That works on a straight ladder. All the wheels can be off the ground, and the weight rests on the outriggers. It didn't sound like a good idea, but everyone was yelling for water. The training representative had told us that the lockdown pins would hold the cab of the truck in position.

The whole cab started to swing around toward me when the outriggers were put further down and the weight of the cab was lifted. A firefighter on the truck put his hands out in an attempt to stop the motion of the cab of the truck.

There wasn't time to bring the outriggers back up, and it looked like this firefighter would be crushed between the outrigger and the cab of the vehicle. Thankfully, the outrigger caught and came to rest on the handrail on the cab of the truck, snapping the handrail off the rear door and putting a crease in the body of the cab where the handrail became pinched. The vehicle was now secure.

The best position of stability when lifting and extending a ladder is to have the ladder jackknifed, which is a ninety-degree angle from the direction you are extending the ladder. It hadn't been planned, but it was accomplished. The ladder was extended to crews waiting on the third floor. Then a water supply was secured for the external ladder pipe.

During the emergency, there was no time to talk about the accident. The master firefighter on the truck told the captain to come talk to me after the fire. The side of the truck facing the fire appeared normal.

Some intoxicated women who had just left a nightclub started yelling praise at me. They liked seeing a female firefighter. They didn't know what had just happened.

During the investigation of the accident, the other shifts admitted they had experienced the cab moving. They had not shared the information and didn't think it was important. It was critical information necessary to avoid having a serious accident or injury.

That is how experience was gained to teach me not to blindly listen to everything directed to do. I realized common sense had to be utilized to make the best decisions. This was hard to do because firefighters are trained to follow orders. The fire service worked much like a military organization. Orders are given through the chain of command. This structure works well in the fire service, especially during emergency operation, so you are taught not to ask questions.

The contradiction for me was that I got in the most trouble when I disregarded my own judgment. When something didn't feel right, it usually wasn't. The expectation to comply with orders contradicted what my conscience told me to do. This was especially hard when the orders were coming from a superior officer.

Another incident occurred because relevant information wasn't shared. When driving responding to a reported structural fire, the hose fell off the truck. The concrete ramp from the station to the street had a dip in it. When the truck hit the dip, the end of the five-inch hose dropped onto the back bumper.

The call was to the right of the station. Calls to the right of the station required the truck to reach maximum speed quickly to cross the overpass close to the station. The truck was heavy, so it was hard to get the speed of the truck up when making a right out of the station.

Although the five-inch hose had fallen off the truck, I checked both mirrors while driving, but the hose couldn't be seen. The speed of driving laid the hose fast. It was airborne and laying straight behind the truck where it couldn't be seen from the mirrors.

The first indication the hose was out of the bed was when the last metal coupling came out of the bed, and hit the right-rear spotlight. The coupling broke the light, and the crashing of glass could be heard. The truck could no longer respond to the call. The house wasn't burning, but our unit had to let the dispatcher know we couldn't respond and to send another unit.

A police car was requested to block the road since the hose in the middle of the street was a hazard. Their vehicle blocked the traffic while the hose was picked up and put back on the truck. Everyone listening to the radio heard what happened. The safety officer responded to take a report because of the damage to the truck. It was embarrassing, but it was frustrating because the other shift had had a problem with the hose connection falling out on the back bumper the day before.

The potential existed for hose to fall off the truck, and daily checks were done to visually check the hose. This incident reinforced its importance. The hose had looked like it was in the hose bed, but the hose hadn't been seated far enough back, and the truck bouncing had worked the hose out of the hose bed and off the truck.

The shift working the day before had laid the hose for a room and content fire. They said the hose had kept coming out of the hose bed after they'd repacked it. They'd failed to take the extra time to repack the hose. The hydrant connection hadn't been put back in the hose bed properly. The driver hadn't mentioned it to me the next morning at shift change. Repacking the hose and passing on the problem would have been the safe and right thing to do.

Fortunately, there had been no cars following too close behind the truck. It was disappointing that the simple act of repacking the hose or telling me about the problem so our shift could repack it could have prevented the accident. No one could see the connection between the hose falling off the truck several times the day before to the incident the next day. It was simply my fault.

Unnecessary accidents happened because of lack of communication. On

Christmas Eve one year, one of our station's engines was sent to the center of the city to backfill due to a large trash-compactor fire at the mall. Shortly afterward, the station's second engine and ladder were dispatched to a fire on the same street. At first, it sounded like units were being dispatched to the same fire at the mall. It sounded like the mall was burning down on Christmas morning. Only the street name was given but not the numerical address, because a car passing by had seen flames.

When our ladder truck came down the interstate, flames could be seen shooting twenty to thirty feet from a two-story office-building roof. Flames were above the steeple of a church that sat in front of the building on fire. Most of the units that would normally respond to this address were already committed to the mall fire. Their fire was challenging because they had to cut the metal sides of the trash compactor to access the densely packed, smoldering paper burning, but this fire was more involved.

The building sat on a road that backed up to the railroad tracks. A captain on one of the trucks already on the scene directed our ladder truck and another engine to cross these railroad tracks to supply their truck with water. This was another example of having to do against an order because common sense said it wasn't a good decision. As the ladder operator responsible for the operation of the truck, my assessment was that it wasn't safe to cross railroad tracks off road. I disobeyed the order. The engine followed the orders and became stuck on top of the railroad tracks.

The point they directed the trucks to cross was off road and not accessible to heavy fire trucks. The sides of the track were built up with gravel, so the tracks were sitting on a hill. There was concern that a train would come and hit the stuck fire truck. The stuck fire truck wasn't in a position to supply the attack truck, so they still didn't have water. The ladder truck was positioned in a small paved area behind the building. It was the only place available that allowed the elevated stream to reach the building.

Water was secured from another fire engine. There were a lot of demands for water to start flowing. As soon as the ladder was supplied with water, the ladder's master stream was directed to the flat rubber-membrane roof with gravel on top where the fire was burning through. To get the water stream in position to hit the main body of fire, the stream had to travel across some of this gravel roof.

The sounds of trucks operating and fire burning that close made it hard to hear radio communications clearly. The battalion chief who responded pulled his vehicle up in the front of the building. He had pulled into a front parking space, so he was too close to the burning structure.

The fire chief responded because it was a large fire and several fires were active at the same time. There were many units working. There weren't many stations not working on one of the fire scenes that Christmas morning. The chief got in the passenger seat with the battalion chief.

The stream from the ladder hit the gravel on the roof and blew it off the other side of the building, hitting the windshield of the vehicle the fire chief was in, breaking the windshield. The battalion chief started yelling on the radio that he was under fire. It was his choice of words because the gravel hitting his windshield sounded like gunfire.

The fire chief came around the back of the building to see which truck was operating the master stream and had inflicted the damage. He only shook his head.

Our ladder truck's master stream had extinguished the largest portion of the fire while the engine was stuck on the railroad tracks. The fire chief's version of the experience was comical. He had to duck and cover his head to avoid windshield glass. My question was why had they parked so close to the building and then ordered the master stream. They knew where the fire was and where the ladder stream was placed. Our crew had missed their radio transmissions over the roar of the fire and the ladder pipe flowing.

The ladder pipe extinguished the majority of the fire. He stated he wasn't surprised who was operating the truck. You couldn't get in trouble doing nothing. I was aggressively in the middle of fire operations. It was my job.

After the fire, a walk around the truck revealed a water can was missing. The water can had sat in a bracket mounted on the diamond plate of the running board of the truck. It wasn't there. The fire had been so large it hadn't been used.

It turned out that the water can bounced off the truck during the long drive on the interstate while responding to the call. It was concerning that the water can had fallen off the truck because a water extinguisher could cause a lot of damage. If it had hit a car going interstate speed, it could have caused an accident and damage to the car. If the water can had hit someone, it had the potential to seriously hurt or kill them.

Another time while driving resulted in a disagreement about the choice to respond to a call the captain made. We had just cleared from the training center from some technical-rescue training. The truck was an old phone-company truck pulling a twenty-four-foot trailer loaded with heavy wood-shoring panels. The truck wasn't designed to pull the trailer with that much weight, but it was the only truck available to our team at the time. There were no funds to purchase a truck, so donated vehicles were utilized. The truck had been given to us because they were receiving a new truck. It was the way technical-rescue team resources had been acquired in the beginning.

When the truck reached the speed of fifty miles per hour, the trailer started fishtailing. It was an emergency vehicle but one that couldn't be pushed past that speed. Another engine was backfilling our station, running calls during our training. Our engine was back at the station. When our crew got back to the station, the engine would be put back into service.

The only unit staffed at the time was an engine. If there was a technical-rescue call, crews moved their gear over and switched trucks. After technical-rescue calls, the engine was placed back in service. The fire training center was about twenty miles from our station. Right after our unit cleared the training center, the captain cleared the backfill engine filling in at our station. It was premature for him to release them.

Right after he released the backfill engine, our station was dispatched to a car fire on the interstate on the far side of our response area. The captain should have told the dispatcher to dispatch another unit closer to the location.

He refused to do it but insisted that the truck be driven faster than the maximum safe speed. He said the car probably wasn't burning—a lot of calls for car fires weren't actually burning—but when we finally arrived, the car was burning. The reports of state troopers on the scene stated the car had only been smoking upon their arrival. The owner of the car wanted to know what had taken the truck so long to arrive.

The car had burned so long it was almost out because all the contents were consumed. Making the suggestion to call for another unit didn't have an effect on the captains' decision. Many times my suggestions were ignored, or others took credit for the idea. My ideas weren't valued or considered in the department. Observing poor decision making taught me to think for myself and make my own size-ups. Confidence in making decisions grew by making consistent good choices, developing my capacity to act independently.

This ability helped me in everyday fire operations. After I was promoted to battalion chief, I was dispatched to a multifamily residential fire on New

Year's Day. The deputy and fire chief responded. The progress of the fire was surprising because the building had sprinklers. The maintenance employee working that day had shut the sprinkler system down because one of the sprinkler heads had been leaking. It was a holiday so the cost to repair the system on a holiday would be more expensive.

A cigarette had been discarded in a planter on a balcony and caught on fire. The fire extended up the outside vinyl siding and entered the soffit and attic space and started to burn the roof off a sixteen-unit apartment building. There were several challenges in this fire; the fact that the fire was well involved upon our arrival was just one of them. There were people watching the fires progress from their balconies instead of evacuating.

When fire units arrived, occupants were trying to move their vehicles. This process of moving cars was blocking the access the fire trucks had to the structure. This apartment complex was on stilts on the first level to provide carports for residents' vehicles. The first real level of living space was on the second floor. Access to apartments was provided by exterior stairs.

The first five-inch supply line blocked access to the fire scene for other emergency vehicles responding. One of the ladder trucks set up too far away for defensive operations to be effective. This was the situation I found upon my arrival.

The first unit that arrived on scene was a fire engine. The deck gun on the top of their truck was used to knock a large amount of the fire down so units could proceed up the exterior stairways to do searches for occupants and to extinguish the fire.

The placement of the ladder truck was ineffective, and they were directed to reposition. Assignments were given to incoming units when the deputy chief arrived on scene. My vehicle was positioned and used as the command post in the center median of a four-lane highway. Many crews were walking up to the command post to receive an assignment upon their arrival because there was a lot of air traffic on the radio.

The deputy chief approached the command post with an open bunker coat, a crooked helmet yelling wildly that I was burning the structure down! He was yelling and screaming uncontrollably on this second-alarm fire. The yelling was so intense, his face was red, and the veins in his neck were distended. If it hadn't been so distracting, it would have been comical. He had no firefighting turnout pants on. His helmet was on, but it sat crooked on his head. Everyone around the command post was surprised by his uncontrolled outburst.

Crews walking up to the command post couldn't understand anything he was saying. The fire was still burning, so orders were given in spite of his ranting. Everyone ignored his presence, even though he was the highest-ranking officer on the scene. He was out of control and not adding anything to the incident. He wasn't giving any orders that hadn't already been given. His presence was distracting and disruptive to incident command.

My strategy was to extinguish the fire and not to let the fire progress. Verbal assignments and directions were given around his display of panic. He was very upset about the placement of the ladder. The correction had already been made, but it took time to bring the ladder down, seat it, bring the outriggers back in, and reposition it. The louder he got, the more controlled and calm my demeanor became, and this only angered him more.

All of the assignments had been made, and now time had to be allowed to let the strategy work. Other chiefs arrived, including the fire chief. They made comments but offered no constructive strategy or tactics. The side of my vehicle became the new command post so I could hear crews' radio transmissions. Senior chiefs didn't take command or improve operations. The fire went out quickly for the situation encountered upon our arrival. The status and progress of the fire had been quickly spreading when units arrived.

The fire chief gave conflicting orders that didn't go through incident command to crews on the fire scene. Lack of a central incident command structure is a contributing factor identified in fire-personnel fatality reports. The fire chiefs conflicting orders proved to be detrimental to the progress of fire extinguishment. The fire chief broke the incident command structure, showing a lack of discipline in following incident command structure.

The deputy chief wanted me to draw a picture of the structure on the command board when he first got there. A picture provided a visual reminder of where fire operations were committed, where crews are operating, and followed the fires progress. I was doing it verbally and mentally in the initial stages because of the urgency of the situation, managing without this drawing as a visual reminder. The fire's location and travel was more than evident, but he needed the visual clues to follow fire operations. There hadn't been time when he'd made the request to stop and provide it to him. My prior experience with him yelling had been so long ago, it hadn't occurred to me he would still manage emergency incidents the same way.

The fire chief came to see me after the fire to talk about some discipline issues with one of my captains. He wanted me to change the discipline so he would be eligible for promotion, even though this captain continued having discipline issues and ended up with more severe discipline in the future. My discipline and this captain's actions didn't stop the fire chief from promoting him.

While there, the fire chief asked me about the recent fire. The opportunity was used to tell him of my concerns about having conflicting orders on an incident scene and the benefits of utilizing the incident command structure. The discussion included the proper discipline required on a fire scene. Conflicting orders from command can have potentially dangerous and fatal outcomes. Conflicting orders from officers not utilizing the incident command system had personally affected me. That is how I learned the importance of a strong incident command system.

It occurred on a large second-alarm commercial fire. Early in my career, a drill had just concluded about crew integrity. Crews had agreed that team integrity was important but had disagreed about some of the situations it could be followed. Following the letter of the law on this fire almost cost me personal bodily harm.

The fire chief had stopped by and told us we had to do everything together, even climb aerial devices when master streams were in operation. This wasn't necessary because the stream could be controlled from the tip or from the turntable below. There was no reason to be in the middle of an aerial device. You were climbing to the top to access a roof or perform some function or in the process of climbing it. There was no reason to stop and remain in between the top and the bottom.

The fire chief was at the fire station when this fire call was received. His orders were fresh and new and couldn't be disregarded. Crews tried to make an interior fire attack, but it was an old structure with many renovations that generated hidden spaces. As part of the ladder crew, we had just gotten off the roof from making a ventilation hole. The fire was not coming through the ventilation hole, because there was a second ceiling past the one penetrated. It was made of wood and plaster and provided a hidden space for the fire to progress.

After the ventilation hole was made, tools were gathered to start the descent down the ladder. It was time to get off the roof because that hidden space was now well involved with fire and the roof showed signs of failure. All crews had evacuated the structure, and the roof was caving in. Units were preparing for defensive operations and were going to start master-stream operations from our ladder. My crew member was at the tip of the ladder, and my position was below him as just directed to do so.

I clipped the ladder belt to the ladder as required when working off the ladder. I had to clip through both sections of the ladder because the rungs were lined up and the clip didn't fit between the rungs. It wasn't safe to move the ladder when someone was secured to the moving sections.

The ladder operator received a conflicting order from a chief who arrived on scene that was different than the original direction given to him by the incident commander. He felt he couldn't disregard the order because it had come from a senior officer. He was a new ladder operator and not familiar with ladder operations. He didn't realize that when he moved the ladder that the ladder sections would pass each other and consider it would be an issue for me.

He gave us no warning he was moving the ladder, so there was little time to disconnect the clip from the ladder before it started moving. The ladder moved slowly enough it gave me time to free the clip from the ladder. My efforts were frantic fumbled attempts to free my clip from the ladder before the sections of the ladder pulled past each other. If I couldn't get the belt clip disconnected, it would have pulled me apart. My captain witnessed the event.

There were so many arguments later about how fire operations went that my near-miss wasn't addressed in the PIA, although it was very personal to me. This experience confirmed the importance of utilizing an organized structured fire incident command system.

The fire chief now still didn't want to hear the criticism and wasn't receptive to its intended message offered about my recent New Year's fire. He was defensive. He had heard about the behavior of the newly promoted deputy chief, but he was protective of him because he had selected him, although he said he would talk to him about it.

Crews joked about the deputy chief's behavior after the fire. One person bowed down on the ground to me for taking his abuse during a stressful situation, complimenting me on continuing to make assignments and remaining focused on fire control and extinguishment while this deputy chief was yelling at the command post. Other battalion chiefs talked about his embarrassing behavior, but everyone knew it would continue.

The fire chief talked to him. The deputy chief made a point to tell me how he had gotten in really big trouble with the chief. He laughed about the scolding. He hadn't gotten into any trouble. The fire chief supported his choice for deputy chief.

This deputy chief had a history of unprofessional behavior on fire scenes. He was the officer who yelled on the actual woman-on-fire call when the truck wouldn't go in pump and there was a delay in getting water. He yelled during the delay. This was my first indication he was unable to control himself under pressure.

He was frustrated and shocked that the source of the fire was a person. He yelled because of his inability to overcome challenges on the emergency scene, and that's how he dealt with his frustration. It still wasn't a pleasant experience to be at the receiving end of one of his frustrated tirades.

The best way I found to control fires both literal and figurative was to rely on my experience and judgment.

CHAPTER TWELVE

Fire Control

Because of the discipline administered to the deputy chief's wife, refusal to falsify training records, or fix promotional process scores, I was transferred out of the training division. Transfers were always justified by referencing departmental need. It was also the known consequences that occurred when you didn't comply with the chief's wishes.

It was unfair, but it represented my resistance to conforming to standard practices that didn't fit with my personal moral integrity. It was retaliatory in nature and delivery since there were other assignments available. A district chief had requested my transfer to his shift, but that request was denied. Others were transferred to ensure my assignment would be in this slow battalion. There would be less work and responsibility, but the pay would remain the same—not a bad deal if unmotivated, but it can feel like a death sentence if you want to be involved.

To give the appearance it wasn't retaliatory, I was promised to be transferred to another battalion during the next transfers. When that didn't happen, I was promised that the transfer would be made when the new promotions were made. When that didn't happen, I was promised the transfer would be made when the reorganization occurred. My transfer finally happened when I became sick from working in that battalion because of recurring mold problems. They said the station didn't have mold, though.

A few years prior to my transfer to the station with mold, my allergies became a problem. Allergy testing was done, and injections started. The station the battalion was housed in had a history of mold problems. One firefighter had been medically discharged from the department due to the exposure to mold in the station he received there. He had seizures and breathing issues. He was ultimately medically disabled from the exposure and medically retired.

The HVAC system had been installed well before the roof was put on. Moisture had gotten into the duct system, and the station had experienced a mold issue ever since. Even firefighters only there on relief had reactions to the mold.

It was noted in every quarterly report submitted by all three of the battalion chiefs assigned there. When I was there only one month, I started getting respiratory infections that couldn't be treated by normal antibiotics. Headaches and skin rashes appeared. It required me to go to the pharmacy for some medicine one night because it was so bad. At my allergy shot appointments, my injection site for mold would get a severe reaction, an indication that there was an exposure to mold. My tolerance for mold was low, and the exposure to the mold was causing the reaction.

I discovered mold in a vent right above the bed I slept in in the battalion chief's bunk room. There was a high use of sick leave from personnel at that station due to respiratory infections. Sick leave use was up on all three shifts. Both other chiefs working there had respiratory infections and had lost time from work due to these infections.

Feeling a responsibility to bring the awareness of the hazards of mold to other firefighters living in that station, I reported my findings to the district chief. He said he contacted the occupational health and safety office.

My doctor put me out on family medical leave for a few weeks to limit my exposure to the mold and to fight the respiratory infections. My symptoms improved in a short time frame, and my doctor concluded that the exposure to mold had occurred at work.

The department said they checked the station for mold and couldn't find any, and they denied having a problem with mold. The ability to fill out an exposure report for being exposed to mold was denied because they said there was no mold present.

A year later, another battalion chief assigned there pressed the issue until a test was conducted to test for mold. Members at that station continued to be sick. That was when I found out that when I made the request to check for mold, no tests were actually done to test if mold was present in the station. The test for mold didn't occur until a year later. That test confirmed there was mold present in the station. Other employees were having respiratory problems so a company was brought in to deal with mold abatement.

But by the time my transfer was granted, I no longer wanted it. The people in the battalion were experienced firefighters. They were some of the best in the department. If the station really didn't have a mold problem, there was no need to transfer me. The responsibility to get the mold problem corrected was greater.

The chief's office said there wasn't a problem with mold at the station but that my transfer needed to occur because of my problems with mold. I was confused because if there wasn't a mold problem at the station, then why did my transfer need to occur.

My time in the battalion had been enjoyable. Many of the members in the battalion were senior employees who had volunteered for the slower assignment to give their bodies a break or who had taken a stand for some injustice in the department. It was a privilege to have earned the transfer to work with other individuals with strong moral integrity.

Transfers there were meant as punishment, but it was a sign of honor. Many other chiefs before me had been transferred there because they had stood up for a just cause. It was an honor to be included in that group.

One particular captain sent to this battalion was the department's most senior employee. Earlier in his career, he had been a captain at an adjoining station to the technical-rescue station when the fire chief had been a captain there. He was an old-school firefighter and had routinely canceled the technical-rescue units responding to calls in his area. The fire chief had held a grudge because of it.

The fire chief had transferred him to this slower battalion. This captain had asked to be transferred back to a busier battalion, but the fire chief had directed the district chiefs to deny the transfer. The chief had said he didn't think the captain was competent. When the captain had asked why the transfer had been denied, one district chief had told him the fire chief didn't have confidence in his abilities.

This had hurt this captain's feelings as he had been a captain longer than the fire chief had been in the department. He'd requested an open door with the chief. An open door was designed as a way an employee could personally talk to the fire chief without having to go through the chain of command. It was allowed if the issue doesn't involve discipline.

The captain had confronted the chief about why he hadn't trusted the captain's abilities. The fire chief had denied saying he thought he'd lacked confidence in the captain, even though several district chiefs had confirmed the fire chief had made the statement.

He told me about the fire chief's lack of truthfulness one night on the front bench at the fire station, not long after my transfer to the battalion. He knew what it felt like to be transferred to the battalion, which was intended to be banishment.

The fire chief was embarrassed he'd gotten caught making statements about this employee. This captain never had any negative documentation in his annual performance evaluations. He was nominated as firefighter of the year before his retirement.

My transfer had been meant to be punishment, but my effort to get transferred out of there was no longer a priority. The reasons for being transferred there were retaliatory, but the assignment was pleasant. The department needed to fix the mold problem at that station and not transfer me because of my reaction to it and just ignore the problem.

The pattern the chief would engage in after someone had disobeyed a request was to build a case against the employee—an offensive tactic in case the employee tried to claim a hostile work environment.

The union president was one of the captains in my battalion. He was the voice for the firefighters' union. The fire chief had made some unpopular decisions in regards to firefighter staffing and safety. He had used vacant firefighter positions to obtain more chiefs to develop a special-operations division. He wanted a battalion chief to individually manage each of the specialty divisions of hazmat, technical rescue, and FEMA. Creating this new division was part of his reorganization plan.

Instead of fighting for a minimum staffing of four on the fire trucks to ensure there was two in and two out to be able to make quick entry into fires, the fire chief pursued the extra chiefs to make the special-operations division. Too many chiefs and not enough firefighters weren't popular with the union. Firefighters make less money than chief officers. More firefighters can be hired for the price of one chief's salary.

The union president's concerns frequently fell on deaf ears, so he took his concerns to the city manager and city council. As a result, he was transferred to this slow battalion. He frequently had district chiefs applying pressure to change some of his positions.

This union president was dispatched to a rescue call for a burn. Details of the call couldn't be heard unless you switched over to the rescue channel. If it was a serious burn injury, this captain would make notifications as outlined in policy.

If there is a serious injury an additional fire truck is dispatched to help in the landing of the critical-care helicopter. The required additional fire truck wasn't dispatched to help land the helicopter on this call to indicate they needed to be airlifted to the hospital and indicate how serious the injuries were.

The patient was an elderly man with Alzheimer's who had been playing with a lighter while sitting in a recliner and had accidently set his shirt on fire. When his shirt had started burning, he'd run out the front door. He'd received serious respiratory and extensive burns to his face.

The house was in a rural area next to a field. The helicopter could land in the field, so there was no need to call for an additional engine. The rescue squad arrived right behind the fire truck and provided the paramedic for the case. That made the rescue department the lead medic on the call. The captain went inside the residence to confirm there was no fire damage to the house.

The rescue paramedic requested the helicopter for patient transport. The fire truck assisted in landing the helicopter, but didn't engage in patient care. The fire unit confirmed there was no fire and, after assisting with loading the patient, went back to the fire station.

The patient's preexisting medical history complicated his condition, and he succumbed to his injuries. The medic on the helicopter was an off-duty firefighter, and he started telling everyone in the fire department about the case.

The next shift the crew at the station told me the details of the case. The ambulance had become stuck in the mud in the field when it had driven the patient out to the helicopter. The rescue unit had requested some lights from the fire crews at the station to clean the mud off the ambulance when they returned.

The death of the patient was caused by fire. I immediately notified the district chief as soon as I found out about it. The fire medic that worked the case off the helicopter made notification up through his chain of command. The deputy chief whose wife I had disciplined was now my supervisor. He started plans for an administrative hearing to discipline me and the union president for not making the proper fire-death notifications.

My call to notify the district chief occurred right before the deputy chief had come into his office. I had made the notification required by policy. I couldn't be disciplined.

Corrective action was made with the captain. Discipline against the union president couldn't be pursued. The way the two departments worked together was a factor in the breakdown of communications. These challenges still face the two departments.

The union president offered to take over the care and maintenance of the fire department's oldest antique fire truck that was in need of repair. The fire chief told the union they could have the truck if this union president would give the department access to one of the volunteer stations. The union president denied the request, so the offer to receive the truck was taken back. They decided to sell it at auction instead.

The union president planned to buy the fire truck at auction, so they took the truck off the market. Ultimately a mutual arrangement was reached. This is the relationship the chief had with the union. If the union president embarrassed the chief, he found ways to retaliate.

The department wanted space in a volunteer station for a rescue unit that this union president controlled, so they wouldn't have to give the rescue department any space in their new building. The new building would become the chief's office, and the chief was relocating the technical-rescue crew into this new building with him. The technical-rescue team had always been his crowning jewel and was to become the centerpiece of this new station, so he didn't want rescue to share space in the new building. To avoid this, he needed the union president to give the rescue department space in this volunteer building he controlled.

Conversations had been ongoing to move the technical-rescue station closer to the center of the city to give them better access. The current station's crew didn't receive the new building but were relocated to accommodate the technical-rescue units even though their response wouldn't be an automatic dispatch through the communications system because it was outside their current assigned area. The transfer was more because the fire chief wanted to reward his technical-rescue team with a new station and who he wanted to be in the station his office would be located in.

So how the fire chief handled situations put me in a defensive mode. My chain of command continued to look for ways to discipline me. One of my stations had a truck maintenance issue that was blown out of proportion.

The captain at the station was on the chief's list to punish because he'd reported a case of sexual harassment against one of his female employees.

The person inflicting the harassment was a battalion chief who was liked and supported by the chief's office. This captain had only been protecting the employee, which was his responsibility as her supervisor. He was interrogated in an administrative hearing as if he was the guilty party. He had strong documentation, but he had been sent to this battalion for his efforts to do what was right and follow policy.

His shift was responsible for maintaining a support vehicle kept in their station for the quarter that rarely responded anywhere. After the maintenance was performed, they drove the vehicle around the block. Starting the vehicle and driving it wasn't required, but they did so because the vehicle was rarely moved.

The next morning, the shift that relieved them noticed a flat spot on one of the tires when they walked by. The captain on the shift was involved in a promotional process. His battalion chief was trying to get transferred out of the slow battalion. The next morning, my district chief insisted a formal investigation start in preparation for an administrative hearing to know why my captain hadn't seen the flat spot on the tire. They said the city garage found metal showing from the tire and didn't believe it could be missed.

The facts were blown out of proportion. My district chief told me the city garage reported the tire was bulging on the side and dry rotted. My district chief said there was no excuse for not seeing it.

I quickly started an investigation with my shift. It was hard for me to believe that they had negligently ignored tire damage when they had gone beyond the requirements to maintenance the truck. They were surprised to hear about the tire's condition since they'd checked the tires during the vehicle maintenance and hadn't noticed the tire bulging. They hadn't checked the tires after they had driven the vehicle around the block, but they had done a good check of them before the vehicle had been driven.

I questioned the mechanic who changed the tire. The main garage had not changed the tire. The truck was taken to the after-hour garage for maintenance because the problem with the tire hadn't been reported until late in the day. If the shift reporting the damage had seen the damage to the tire in the morning, why had they waited all day to take the truck to the garage? If it was such a big safety concern, it was unusual that the truck wasn't immediately taken to the garage to be fixed.

The night mechanics came on duty at four o'clock in the afternoon. The mechanic who had changed the tire was consulted to get the details of the tires damage. The mechanic was surprised that a chief was there to inquire about the tire. He showed me the tire. He had to retrieve it from the debris dumpster at the main garage, but the tire was required to conduct the required investigation.

Without the tire inflated, there was no bulge in the tire. The mechanic said there was about a two-inch, slightly raised bubble on the tire when inflated. He said it would be very hard for firefighters to see this bubble because the spot was on the inside of the outside rear dual tire. The bubble would have faced away from the outside and been in the two-inch gap between the two tires. He asked if someone was trying to get the firefighter in trouble.

I asked him if the tire had to hit anything to sustain this type of failure. He said the tires just separate when they fail without warning. He said there was no dry rot or exposed metal from the tire. The tire could have failed due to age. All the tires were put on at the same time, so he changed all of them.

The main garage had performed the annual maintenance of the vehicle about six months prior. No tires had been ordered or put on the vehicle. The vehicle's mileage put on the vehicle in a year was low. The vehicle only got driven around the block or went to the annual inspection at the garage. Most of the miles on the tires since the last inspection were from the drive to the garage to have the tires changed.

The captain was uncomfortable because of the investigation leading to an administrative hearing. He'd been involved with one before. This tire had failed while parked at the station. When the vehicle was moved, the tire stopped in a different place and the spot on the tire could be seen from the rear. The report to document the findings of the investigation consisted of several pages.

The city garage had inspected the truck six months before and had not noted any tire damage. The mileage on the vehicle and age of the tires didn't qualify the vehicle for new tires, but the tire had separated sitting in the bay of the station. The recommendation was to amend the vehicle check off to include a tire check after the vehicle was driven. I recommended no discipline be administered.

My investigation didn't warrant the discipline senior staff wanted to administer. They had been convinced by listening to secondhand information that there was a conspiracy to cover up damage to the tire. They were prepared to administer discipline, but my report didn't support it.

This small incident turned into a labor-intensive investigation. That's how issues were handled in the department. The micromanagement style of leadership and lack of trust of employees generated slow progress on issues that should have been handled quickly. Senior chiefs lacked the interpersonal skills to work with other departments in the city. Their failure to cultivate relationships with other departments was a deterrent to the working relationship with them.

This example is just one of the incidents that occurred. There were many where routine functions turned into unnecessary and time-consuming projects. Senior management found fault with individuals who hadn't broken policies but didn't discipline others who clearly had. They repeated patterns that provided insight on what the probable outcome would be.

After undeserved discipline, senior staff launched justification campaigns as strategies to explain questionable behaviors. They prepared defense cases ahead of time. During promotional processes, discipline was administered to people participating in the process to make them ineligible for promotion and ensure preselected choices would be promoted.

They also reduced the minimum qualifications required for the position before the promotional process started. The educational requirements were lowered. People were put in acting roles they weren't qualified for. Promotional processes were postponed until preferred applicants met the written qualifications to participate in the process. Certifications were eliminated if their selections didn't have them.

My current district chief was the best man in the wedding of the deputy chief whose wife worked at the training center, so they were friends. He talked in the morning battalion meetings and criticized training that had been conducted while I had been chief there during our morning chiefs' meetings. He stated current operational issues were my fault as the training chief at the time. It became a joke among the other battalion chiefs. It became so obvious that whenever anything went wrong in operations, everyone jokingly pointed at me and said it was my fault because it hadn't been taught in training during my tenure there.

One accusation was that the child safety seat (CSS) recertification wasn't scheduled. That program fell under fire education and the fire marshal's office. They worked on site in schools. They were the contact between the insurance agencies and the certifying agency for the CSS training. The lead educator was the instructor, and I talked to him about scheduling the class when I was chief of training because he was the contact and provided the instructors for the program.

I blocked some time out on the calendar to ensure they had space for the training, and gave him the dates. He neglected to make contact with the licensing agency and schedule a class. His failure to schedule the training suddenly became my fault.

My job as the training chief was to plan necessary training and provide opportunities and space for the training to occur. Scheduling department training was done through the staffing officers in fire operations.

I remember one particularly challenging call while working in the slow battalion after my transfer from fire training involved a brush fire. A large column of black smoke was coming from the rural part of my response area. While I was driving through neighborhoods, trying to find the source of the smoke, I saw a district chief outside his house. He wanted to know what was going on. I pointed out the black column of smoke and told him the location of the source was being investigated. My area had several active agricultural burn permits, but none of them were in the area of this column of smoke.

It was unusual there hadn't been any calls about it yet, but one was received soon afterward. I directed a fire unit to check the address the complaint call was received from, and directed the next responding engine dispatched to check another area. I requested a tactical channel from the dispatcher so I could coordinate fire units' efforts since more fire units were assigned to the case.

A resident who had been four wheeling in the area came out to my vehicle. He stated that there were a lot of paths leading back to the area on fire, but nothing a truck could fit down. He said some juveniles were back there hiking. The fire was back in these woods.

That's why I requested more fire units and brush trucks. These trucks are designed to go off road and carry water and pump and drive at the same time. This off-duty district chief rode back to assess the situation with an off-duty firefighter on a motorcycle. Some fire crews walked back to assess what and how much was burning to get an indication of what other resources would be required to extinguish the fire.

It took a while to walk back to where the fire was located. It was dense with trees and far off the road. The area was marshy, and firefighters were sinking in mud with every step. There was one access road used by the forestry department that brush trucks tried to drive on, but the trucks quickly became stuck.

Firefighters had to cut trees down to get back to the area. A four-wheel vehicle was requested to access the area. There was a small, shallow waterway that one of the flat-bottom boats could navigate. If the fire was close enough to the waterway, the boat could be used with a portable pump to try and extinguish the fire. We still couldn't locate the fire, and we couldn't determine the direction of travel.

The police helicopter was out of service, so there was no air support. The aerial view could have identified the direction and progression of the fire. The department of forestry's response was requested. They have big bulldozers that can push down trees and make trenches around the burning area. The fire could then be contained so it would burn out.

Our department had neglected to sign the mutual aid agreement with the department of forestry. They had notified our department that they wouldn't respond until this agreement was signed. It was sitting on the desk of one of the newly promoted district chiefs who wasn't proficient in administrative work. He'd proved this by not even getting his own application for promotion in on time.

Resources were limited. The resources available were ill equipped to handle a brush fire this large. Our department had access to grant money to purchase new brush fire equipment, but it was used for the technical-rescue team instead.

There were plenty of personnel, but they couldn't get to the fire. The brush trucks couldn't gain access to the area. The equipment on the brush trucks was limited. It was hard to get water to the fire. The trucks couldn't reach the area burning. The equipment that was available was hand carried by firefighters. The water way couldn't be utilized because it was too far away from the fire.

The help of another chief officer wasn't required because of the district chief on scene, but an off-duty firefighter relayed a message that this district chief left. This was going to be a long, labor-intensive incident. It wouldn't be the type that won awards or got media attention like the jet crash.

The most senior captain was the first one to make it back to the area. He'd been sinking knee deep with every step because the fire was in the marsh. His first assessment was that the fire could be put out with a water can, which holds five gallons of water.

His position was under heavy tree cover. The column of black smoke was getting larger. A local news helicopter reported forty acres burning. That was larger than a five-gallon water can could put out.

My district chief responded to the scene. The situation wasn't ideal. A couple of crews were around the command post, waiting for a ride on one of the four-wheelers responding. When my district chief arrived, he started to yell and criticize my fire operations strategy.

It was a demeaning and an unproductive display of his frustration. He didn't offer any constructive usable ideas to make the incident better. He was ignorant of the challenges. The decisions made at his administrative level had caused some of the challenges. Those decisions prevented us from having the resources to effectively attack the fire.

The crews around the command post heard his outburst. They were exhausted from hauling gear back and forth in the woods. It was starting to get cold and dark. They walked over to give me verbal updates about the fire. They were rude in how they addressed the district chief. They didn't appreciate his lack of respect and appreciation for their efforts to put this difficult fire out.

He was surprised that he wasn't well received, but he only received the same treatment and respect he extended to working crews. I asked him to move to another access point to get a different perspective. It distanced him from crews before they got in trouble for insubordination. It also got him away from my command post.

This encounter made me calm on the outside but livid inside. His behavior was expected, but it was still hard for me to tolerate. My concern was that crews would see my lack of response as a sign of weakness. Experience had taught me not to engage in unprofessional behavior on an emergency scene.

Later, I communicated to him that his conduct was not appreciated on the emergency scene. He told me it was his prerogative as my senior officer.

As soon as I had confirmation that the fire was headed toward the marsh, I terminated fire operations. There was a change in the wind direction, and the fire was going to be allowed to burn. There was nowhere for the fire to go. I made the decision without his approval.

Crews would still be there for several hours, picking up equipment. A tow truck had to respond to pull out the stuck brush trucks.

Periodically I directed fire units to check the area during the night to ensure conditions hadn't changed, and I checked the area again the next morning.

The next morning was the monthly staff meeting. I had spent most of the night at the brush fire. I looked forward to attending the meeting to discuss the problems encountered on this fire. How I approached talking about the incident was critical. They were already looking for any reason to discipline me, so I was careful that nothing that was said could sound like insubordination.

The deputy chief couldn't understand why all those units were out there on a brush fire when the senior captain had said it could be put out with a water can. He trusted the judgment of a junior officer over mine. The aerial news footage confirmed the fire was at least forty acres and clearly larger than a water can fire.

Everyone was joking about the incident the next morning. It was an impossible situation with the challenges that existed. My focus was to correct the deficiencies our department had in responding to these types of large brush fires. Members of the battalion had identified the deficiencies in the past, but no action had been taken to correct the problems.

I offered ideas on the use of grant money and a mutual aid agreement with the department of forestry. The discussion went on long enough to make the decision to form a committee to address some of the concerns. The opportunity presented itself to embarrass my district chief in front of his peers as he had extended the curtsey the night before to me during this staff meeting.

I repeated some of his comments to give the fire chief an opportunity to correct any discrepancies. The comments were shallow and didn't add anything to the positive outcome of the fire. No apologies or acknowledgments of their unrealistic expectations with the current resources were made. They were never wrong, no matter what, and they never apologized or made any corrections about their misconceived opinions.

It was exhausting trying to make suggestions to improve the department with the challenges presented to me. The ability to perform my job was becoming increasingly difficult. The resources and support to do so weren't available. The battle to avoid senior chief's retaliation was time consuming. It was becoming a losing battle.

I was eligible to retire. After consideration and conducting a thorough size-up, I determined it was safer to retire than to risk discipline or demotion that would affect my retirement.

Senior staff had a history of retaliation, and the current threat to me was real. It was exhausting evaluating even routine decisions that were basic elements of the job. It was a distraction that could cause me to lose focus on real life-and-death decisions required on emergency scenes. Firefighter and civilian safety should be the focus, not defensive tactics to avoid undeserved discipline. This fire was growing out of control.

Senior staff's petty criticisms were not worthy of the time and effort required to address them. Emergency services require complete focus. They were making it increasingly hard to focus and were robbing me of the joy of working in the fire service. Even though their retaliatory efforts were a known tactic of theirs to get members to leave the department, my strategy was to retire to maintain a career free of discipline, but on my own terms.

CHAPTER THIRTEEN

Fully Involved

Another example of retaliation came during a conversation about the current use of sick leave in our department. Since I was heavily involvement in department scheduling and staffing, the deputy chief asked for my opinion. He was trying to understand the problem. His wife and brother were two of the heaviest abusers of sick leave. The sick leave usage was high in the department. About fifteen people were calling out sick every day. There were about that many annual leave spots available, but with long-term injuries and vacancies, the department had limited the amount of leave spots available. The increase in sick-leave usage was the response to the lack of available annual leave.

The value of sick leave was only about a dollar an hour upon payout at retirement, so people at the end of their careers used a lot of sick leave. The annual leave was saved and taken as a lump-sum bonus because it was paid at your current salary upon retirement. The deputy chief asked me what I thought the real problem with the abuse of sick leave was.

My opinion was if the value of sick leave was increased, there would be a decrease in its use. If sick leave was worth more at retirement, employees would take better care of it and not abuse it. The result would be a decrease in the use of sick leave and a decrease in the amount of overtime to staff the positions created by those calling out sick. The department was already spending extra money for overtime to cover the vacancies caused by people calling out sick. If sick leave was paid at its current value, it wouldn't be more than the money paid for overtime due to the abuse of it. Overtime is paid at time and a half. This could help correct the abuse of sick leave.

When my district chief heard my explanation, he told me the solution shouldn't have been offered. He disagreed with my position. He said that sick leave was never designed to be a benefit for an employee. He said it was just a bulk of leave paid at the end of your career to help you get to the first retirement check.

My husband had retired from the city once before to take a chief's job in another state, and we didn't have to wait for his first retirement check. The lump sum of sick leave was never considered as an option or benefit at retirement.

He said sick leave wasn't a benefit for employees and told me the opinion shouldn't have been shared. Sick leave is actually a benefit for city employees to utilize for long- and short-term illness. The request was from a senior officer. He asked me because of the experience gained from doing staffing and tracking sick-leave usage.

The district chief was asked why viable solutions weren't valued. He just didn't value or want to hear my solutions. The deputy chief asked a direct question. To not answer or offer solutions was negligent.

He said the deputy chief had already decided what the remedy was, which was to increase the number of leave spots so crews would stop using sick leave. Basically, he had already decided on a remedy my suggestion didn't support, which proved his remedy less effective. As I predicted, even though the available leave spots were increased, the sick leave continued.

More leave spots were good for firefighters. The value of sick leave remained the same, so it was still utilized. The increase in leave spots didn't affect the amount of sick leave taken.

My position required me to evaluate current issues and function at a higher level. There was an obligation to perform administratively and operationally. The responsibility and accountability for the safety of citizens and personnel was just one aspect of the job.

My position and approach to solutions to problems was different, so they weren't valued or appreciated. They were generally attacked. They didn't fit in with the senior-staff logic. They were defensive about alternative solutions even if better for the department. Ultimately, you were punished for having individual ideas, even though these decisions might produce the best outcome. I followed their direction if I didn't find it unethical, but a lot of their desires were only communicated to a few.

Senior staff didn't include or utilize their chief officers as they are designed to operate. Many problems went unresolved. No actions to correct problems were allowed unless senior staff approved it. The intentions of senior staff were secret, so no one could help them. But they didn't want help. Their hidden agendas only made others suspicious of their intentions. Only a few select individuals were allowed in their inner circle. They were the only ones who knew the chief's vision, and they would later become senior staff.

All of my evaluations were good and exceeded the requirements. Senior staff appeared intimated by my abilities or didn't understand my position and questioned my loyalty because I was unwilling to sacrifice my integrity. My education, common sense, hard work, and integrity became stumbling blocks that prevented me from being included in their inner circle.

Their tactic was to limit individual's opportunities to participate in projects that possessed the highest capability to the job. Preventing these individuals from participating in projects limited their capacities to improve the organization and their abilities to give different points of view on some bad decisions. Their strategy contained the fire and passion of individuals. It limited their ability to utilize the expertise they possessed.

Senior staff perceived exceptional employees as a threat. They surrounded themselves with people similar to themselves. Anyone who made them feel inferior was excluded from helping in the programs and growth of the department.

Diversity wasn't embraced in the department; it was feared. Because they didn't understand a different perspective and were unwilling to consider it, they didn't consider the alternative. Because the position was different than theirs, they labeled it as wrong.

The personal attacks on me would come unprovoked and as a surprise. During one morning meeting, the conversation included discussion about the delivery of new Suburbans that would replace older, existing battalion vehicles. The new vehicles would provide a vehicle for the three new special-operations battalions.

The topic included their vehicle numbers and radio designations. There were two additional battalion numbers and vehicles that allowed off-duty battalions to return to work during large-scale events. The three new special-operations battalions required three new battalion designation numbers. The current assignments would require higher numbers be used for the new battalion chief's designation.

The fire chief did not want the special-operations battalions to have high designation numbers. He requested the current thirteen battalions to reorganize to accommodate them having lower designation numbers. The lower numbers were perceived as more prestigious and important. They would also receive the newer vehicles even though they wouldn't be responding to emergency incidents.

This was insignificant and not in line with the strategic vision or goals of the department. My opinion wasn't shared because it would be viewed negatively. The conversation switched to the topic of transfers, which included the transfer of one of my employees.

A prior ten-year employee had resigned to pursue another job as a boat captain. He had changed his mind and wanted to return to the department. His medical certifications had expired, and he had to retest to retain his medical certification required for his reinstatement. He was to return to the same station prior to his separation from the department. To accommodate this, someone else needed to be transferred.

The assignment was a slower station but one he'd requested prior to his separation from the department. My stations had the highest vacancy rate because the most senior employees worked there and retired. An arrangement was made to transfer a one-year employee out of that station to a busier station to accommodate the return of this employee. This would give that person an opportunity to gain experience at a station that ran more calls.

The reinstated employee didn't want to go back to his old assignment. I didn't feel someone requesting reinstatement should be particular about where they are assigned and get that much input on their reinstated assignment. It also would help a current, less experienced firefighter.

The battalion receiving the transferred firefighter wanted the one-year employee. During the discussion, the district chief told me it was no different than my husband coming back to the department after he'd retired. He said I should consider the similarity next time I was in bed with my husband. His response shocked me. My husband had retired after thirty years to gain a higher rank in another fire department out of state. He'd been gone from the department for a year. The other department was hit hard by the recession. He'd been faced with firing two local long-term employees in that department. Instead of firing them, he resigned. His vacated position was used to save their positions.

He returned to his employment with our department. He possessed experience that could be taught to others. He didn't ask for a special assignment upon his return. One situation was nothing like the other.

My response was that the situations weren't comparable or relevant to each other. He repeated the comment in an unprofessional, attacking manner.

The more agreeable and accommodating my response was, the stronger the efforts to attack me became. It was an unprovoked personal attack. Others in the meeting, who witnessed the attack, later apologized for his behavior because it was so blatant and embarrassing.

Senior staff judged employees' performances by how well they liked you. It was a subjective assessment. Their assessments were rarely based on facts. They were based on associations made at private social events.

The challenge to be invited stemmed from the nature of the entertainment engaged in. They attended sporting events, campouts, and trips to gentlemen's clubs. This usually prohibited my participation.

A contributing factor to inclusion to the group was membership in the USAR FEMA team. The fire chief was assigned as a captain at the technical-rescue station when the FEMA team was formed. Both deputy chiefs at the time had been captains there, and a majority of the district chiefs had worked at that station. I was not extended inclusion into this group even though I had also been assigned to that station and team from the beginning.

Tackling tough issues was perceived as not being a team player. The response was defensive if you attempted to address tough issues. My assessment was that they were intimidated and fearful of addressing these issues and resisted change. Their reaction was to punish anyone who tackled the problems they wanted to avoid.

Ignoring tough issues and just fitting into the norm was rewarded. Remedies presented to correct problems were rejected. If your solution or perspective was different than theirs, you were prevented from working on the problem.

Early in my career, there weren't opportunities to voice concerns to bring change. My rank provided the opportunity, but the message wasn't received. Speaking up was perceived as a threat and a cause to discipline me.

I realized this fire was fully involved and couldn't be extinguished. All the strategy and tactics attempted were ineffective. This fire was burning out of control. Even defensive tactics weren't effective. My risk-benefit analysis revealed there was nothing more worth saving.

CHAPTER FOURTEEN

Mayday

I responded to fires no matter where assigned, even when assigned in what was considered the slow battalion. People questioned whether they were in the right battalion when running calls with me. Sometimes my battalion ran the most calls on my shift. One call would be cleared only to receive another one. The slow assignment meant to be punishment became fun and enjoyable. The intended outcome hadn't worked out as senior staff had planned. There was a house fire within the first few shifts.

Senior chiefs always have the option to respond to fires, but many were small, single-family residential fires that didn't even require a second battalion officer. This particular fire was in a small apartment above a detached garage away from the house. Several senior chiefs from the office responded.

They lacked discipline because they responded to small fires instead of completing crucial administrative duties. Mutual aid agreements went unsigned. Instead, they chased fires that already had sufficient resources to handle. Their intent may have been to form relationships with crews, but instead it communicated a lack of trust in crews' abilities.

A district chief responded to one of my fires but only took an indirect although active role in its outcome. He and only two of the dispatched fire units were on scene upon my arrival. He didn't take a forward position but roamed around freely without an assignment. The occupant had used fireworks the night before. Everyone inside was sound asleep. There were no working smoke detectors.

A police officer who covered that area had decided to patrol the long strip of road one last time before he got off duty. He saw flames and thought someone had started a large bonfire. When he approached the scene, he realized the house was on fire. He quickly called the dispatcher to report the fire. Then he started beating on the door to alert the occupants because the fire was progressing quickly.

He couldn't get a response from anyone inside, but there were cars in the driveway. He forced the front door open, woke up the occupants, and assisted them outside. If he hadn't alerted the occupants and gotten them outside, they would have been seriously hurt.

Fire trucks arriving could see flames from a long distance. When the fire department arrived on scene, the house was well involved with fire. The flames were burning through the roof. Crews made an interior fire attack.

The district chief freely roaming around on the scene reported the fire under control to me at the command vehicle. I didn't think the color and amount of smoke indicated the fire was extinguished.

He insisted I relay the status of fire under control over the radio to the dispatcher. He knew senior staff were listening to the call, and he wanted to give the quick under-control status to alleviate concern.

Confident the fire was out, he prepared to leave. The fire wasn't out. It had extended into the attic space. It had shown its hidden location and now was burning through the roof. Elevated defensive master streams from the ladder had to be utilized to extinguish the fire.

He was concerned about what I said next on the radio. Confidence in my crew's ability to get the fire under control quickly delayed my radio transmission. There was no need to alarm anyone listening on the radio. He was relieved a change in status wasn't broadcast.

He was anxious and worried. He had insisted on giving the status of fire under control, but I still had the responsibility for the mistake as the incident commander. Thankfully, crews were competent and quickly handled the emergency.

If the fire was intensifying or unable to be extinguished, I would have to make the correction of the status of the fire on the radio, but conflicting fire reports are confusing. Actively fighting fire does not come after a fire-under-control status. The district chief was more worried about the mistake in fire conditions being found out than in the actual emergency.

The deputy police chief called the police officer who located the fire and had him make an immediate report of the incident. The deputy chief's main concern was if the officer had told the dispatcher he was going inside the residence. He was trying to keep his officers safe and ensure they didn't take unnecessary risks. He was also concerned about a police officer taking on duties outside his level of training.

He had told the dispatcher. It was important to know if he hadn't come out. There had been some problems with police officers parking their vehicles in front of fire scenes and blocking fire apparatus. But the police officer had actually parked his car so far away that the fire truck almost passed the house on fire. They were looking for the police car's lights, but the car was parked around the corner from the house on fire.

Firefighters complained when police officers make fire rescues. It wasn't the police department's job. They didn't have the protective equipment or training to make entry to house fires, but in this case, the officer had done the right thing. The progress of the fire was too involved to wait for fire unit's arrival. His decision to complete another check of the area saved lives.

The district chief who came to this fire was given direction from the fire chief to respond to every fire because of his micromanagement leadership style, but crews responding were more than capable of handling and managing the call, while the district chief who had responded to this call had less fire operational experience than I did. He wasn't the best person to make decisions about fire operations, but he was the highest-ranking officer on the scene. He looked for opportunities to demonstrate his authority, especially on high-profile calls. He had been one of the first senior officers on the large jet crash our city experienced.

The jet crash occurred during a weekday afternoon during spring break when all the children were out of school. The pilot obviously didn't have school-age children or he would have known it was spring break and the children were out of school. He later said he purposely avoided crashing into the school and tried to make it to the ocean. He was unable to get there and crashed into an apartment complex instead.

The pilot had somehow managed to put the jet down in the center courtyard of a grouping of apartments. When the first fire unit arrived and gave their initial status of the situation found, you could hear the engine from the jet that had broken off the wing of the plane still turning and roaring in the background.

Jet fuel had spilled and ignited. There were three separate apartment buildings in the grouping on fire. The first truck took the apartment most involved with fire. The truck that responded with them took the next involved, and the third engine that arrived took the remaining building on fire. Generally, one such occupancy would get six trucks. On this event each building only got one crew until more fire units arrived on the scene.

The pilot had ejected at the last possible moment and was assisted freeing himself from his parachute by an administrative member of the fire department who had arrived on scene. His first concern was for the occupants of the apartment building. Miraculously, no one was seriously injured or killed.

Everyone working on that call did a good job with the situation found upon their arrival. Single fire units were assigned whole apartment buildings due to the lack of initial resources available. A large area was affected by burning fuel and fire from the jet fuselage. The jet crash occurred on a fire recruit burn day. A fire engine from a nearby station was helping as safeties in the burn building. The jet crash was in their response area.

The captain riding in the position of battalion chief came by the burn building to watch the recruits during the burn evolutions. He was going to receive one of the recruits at his station. We hadn't seen each other since a particular large incident we'd both responded to years before.

Those fires had involved coastal properties that had been built very close together. The fire had spread from the originating home to six other houses. There had been several other homes with heavy damage, including some cars. The homes had been in such close proximity to each other that the fire leapfrogged to the next one quickly. High winds in excess of thirty-five miles per hour had intensified the fire.

There had been more than one unit on fire, so it had been hard to judge which unit the fire had originated from. The fire had been so intense and the wind so strong that the flames had extended to the roofs of several houses across the street.

As the captain and I talked, we discussed how there hadn't been a fire that large in a while.

The next recruit evolution started, and he left. The evolutions lasted about twenty minutes. Near the end of the evolution, I heard a loud explosion. The training center was next to two military bases that frequently performed maneuvers. Special-operations teams worked nearby. Initially, the noise was attributed to something they were doing.

There had been a fire in one of their training facilities before. The fire had been really hot and the smoke really black due to the walls being covered with foam insulating material. The contents of their structure contained a lot of ammunition. During this fire, explosives were going off.

A check on the radio after hearing this loud explosion revealed the dispatch of a jet crash about four miles from our location. Fire units were routinely sent to standby for aircraft experiencing engine trouble. Those calls rarely resulted in an actual crash. Because of the audible confirmation and multiple calls, the crash was quickly confirmed.

The fire engine helping us was released to respond. It was in their first-due response area. The captain in charge of the recruits was directed to hydrate, rest, and rehab the recruits. Their assistance would be needed at the emergency scene. They weren't certified firefighters yet, but they could be used for support functions.

An event of this magnitude would quickly deplete the city's resources. Everyone was more interested in responding to the call than in supporting the operation. Three reserve fire engines were kept at the training center. I directed the other captain assigned there to coordinate with resource management to get the needed equipment to make the trucks ready to be able to run emergency calls.

The reserve fire engines at the training center didn't have all the needed equipment and weren't ready to run calls. They had to be quickly equipped with excess equipment at resource management.

These challenges prevented the reserve training engines from being ready to go into service right away. The quarterly fire chief meeting with the captains was scheduled to be held on this day in the auditorium at the training center. They were available to staff these additional fire engines at the training center and go into service to run calls. Other reserve engines were located and put into service with available personnel at the training center.

One of the challenges of a large emergency incident was the strain it puts on the entire system. An incident the size of a jet crash strained the emergency system. It couldn't keep up with the normal influx of emergency calls throughout the city. All units were dispatched to this incident, which didn't leave any other units to run the normal call volume.

Mutual aid was automatically requested from neighboring cities. Part of this challenge was that not all cities worked on the same radio system, so it limited their ability to communicate.

I notified the district chief's office of the equipment available for assignment. I then put myself into service to run emergency calls. This was done on my own initiative without direction. The natural inclination is to run to the fire and see the excitement, and is generally what happens. Everyone responded to the fire. This left me to run calls for the entire city.

There was a paging system to notify off-duty chiefs of working incidents. The problem with the system is that it was antiquated. No one carried a pager anymore. The paging system had the capability to send alerts to cell phones, but few chiefs were issued department cell phones.

Eventually two battalion chiefs returned to duty, but only one vehicle was available. There were few resources to run the remaining calls in the city. Right after I went in service, I received a call. The district chiefs had limited the ability of a battalion chief to modify the response of emergency vehicles. It was done when there is a high volume of calls or lack of resources. Both were the case.

A battalion chief can essentially limit unit's response by canceling every unit they don't want responding, but it generates a lot of work for the dispatcher. They have to find and recommend units to respond. Under the circumstances, I ordered the dispatcher to go to a modified response, even though it could be grounds to discipline me. The dispatcher was relieved and thanked me over the air. They were already having a difficult time finding units to fill out the recommended response.

Thankfully, none of my superior officers heard me give the order to the dispatcher for the modified response. It was ridiculous to consider this an issue worthy of discipline, but senior chiefs had made it an important issue. It was another sign of the micromanagement leadership style the chief demanded. It was the right thing to do, but it could still have resulted in discipline. The threat was real because there was an active effort to find a reason to administer discipline to me.

When a mutual aid truck responding from another city announced their response, they were added to the available units even though they hadn't arrived yet. They started getting dispatched to calls.

I did not have a computer in my vehicle, which meant I couldn't refer to the address and units responding but had to manage incidents only by what the dispatchers broadcast. Comments other than the address and units responding from the dispatcher were no longer broadcast because they were written in the case comments on the computer.

Case comments would have been helpful to decide the likelihood of an actual fire to determine if some units responding could be canceled to run another of the many calls that were starting to be dispatched. The computer could check vehicle location or where a unit had been assigned.

Before the direction to the dispatcher to go to a modified response, a call for a boater in distress was dispatched at the same time as a fire alarm. The dispatcher assigned me to both calls. Boat calls were lengthy. It took a while for the fireboat to arrive at the site of a boat in distress.

Then my unit was dispatched to a structural fire. The few units available were quickly depleted. The dispatcher called for assistance because no units were left to respond. Cases were prioritized, and units were cleared and diverted to higher priority calls.

Rearranging units was challenging without knowing where units were responding from. Calls were happening right after another because the dispatcher had to hold calls. Without a computer, I had to record calls the old-fashioned way—by writing them down. This was challenging when trying to drive at the same time.

While I was pulled over to write an address and responding units down, an intoxicated homeless woman started knocking on my window. It was an unwelcome added distraction.

The dispatcher referred media calls to me. Our PIO was on the scene of the fire engaged in fire operations. One media call was from an international news station. Calls continued until after midnight.

Eventually, an off-duty captain came back to duty to drive for me. He anxiously wanted to go by the scene of the jet crash. He was in a promotional process and wanted to get involved in fire operations. Units had been on the scene several hours, and the fire was out. There was no operational need to go by the incident.

Our responsibility was to run calls. Our response area covered one hundred and fifty square miles. Crews operating on the scene had to recon and wash their fire gear when finally relieved on the scene. Their gear had toxic materials and jet fuel on it, which is cancer causing.

Crews after the incident discussed how senior staff weren't protected at the scene, lacking their protective clothing or breathing apparatus. Operational crews were in complete PPE and breathing apparatus. Crews joked that the fire chief and his staff must have a secret air bubble around them because they stood out in the middle of the scene with no protective equipment on.

If they had participated in the jet crash training just completed, they would have heard the military state the importance of personal protection. The particles that jets are made of are highly toxic. Even small particles when ingested or inhaled are harmful. There were big particles floating through the air. The safety officer filled out an exposure report for the whole department for this incident because at one point or another we were all there.

The captain who came by the training center during the recruit evolution was the first incident commander on the scene. He had done a good job, sounding calm on the radio as he gave his initial report. The whine of the jet engine that was still turning could be heard in the background. He was complimented on the direction he'd given incoming crews. His initial command and control of the incident provided the command structure for the entire incident. The incident had gone smoothly, especially under the circumstances. He never got any credit for his efforts.

The first senior officer who'd arrived wrote fire journal articles and went on tours to talk about the incident command system he'd set up. His account left very little credit for those first crews who actually set up the incident command system.

The first senior officer had done a good job on the incident but capitalized on the incident without giving credit to the first officers who'd set up the incident command's success. His article made it sound like he had been the only one making critical decisions. If a critique of the incident had been completed, it would have identified other's efforts.

Those first crew's initial actions had made the search-and-rescue efforts successful. The strategy the first incident commander had built was the command structure the incident had run on. Those efforts had made the incident a success. This chief would go on to teach about his incident command structure at fire conferences.

A critique didn't occur in the department because our department was too busy pursuing national attention. They forgot about the members of our own department, even though almost every fire unit in the city responded to the incident. It would be challenging to have all units attend a critique, but the first alarm units that responded could have conducted a critique to discuss lessons learned.

The video department had the capability to provide a live feed video to get member participation and fulfill the challenge of allowing everyone to participate.

Finally, after crews complained about not conducting a critique, a live video was used to review the incident, but it was a year later. The participation was poor because of the delay and how it was handled. Very few people participated when the live broadcast occurred. The effect of the perceived slight had changed members' motivations to participate.

Crews wanted leaders to recognize and include them so they could learn together. They wanted to review the incident to understand which strategies worked. It was the mechanism to become better and more prepared for the next incident. They were not afforded this opportunity.

By the time a critique was attempted, the attitude of the members was poor because they didn't feel valued. They were the first to respond to the incident, but they were the last to be asked to participate in a critique.

It is a great idea to share lessons learned with as many people as possible, and a department critique of the incident should have been a high priority. Someone on limited duty finally compiled the written after-action reports from all units that responded. There was no final disposition provided to crews working at the incident that submitted input. Later, the report was coincidentally located in a remote archive electronic file.

Senior staff was too late in their realization they had left the most important people out. They were too busy receiving praise. Senior staff's behavior was a topic of ridicule for fire operations personnel. Their vision and focus was so narrow they missed what was going on around them.

It is easy to judge others, but as a leader, you should lead by example.

Not one person lost his or her life in the jet crash, even with the extensive damage to the apartment complex.

No one realized the support efforts that were required. When problems identified with the system were shared to try to correct them, the ideas presented to improve them were ignored. The senior chiefs didn't want to listen to the concerns.

There was a better way to notify off-duty personnel. There were some logistical equipment needs that should have been addressed. The existing command vehicles needed additional equipment to make them functional. Mine and others suggestions weren't well received.

Suggestions and remedies to improve operations only resulted in being transferred.

CHAPTER FIFTEEN

Fire Out

I experienced other frustrations even after my transfer back to a busier battalion. Senior staff had tried to keep the reorganization of response areas such a secret they didn't run the idea by the operational battalion chiefs first. They picked a day to make the change, but neglected to include the emergency dispatch center or operational battalion chiefs in the planned changes.

They changed the stations the battalion chiefs were responsible for, but the dispatcher was still dispatching them with their old stations. They neglected to include the department that dispatched the calls. The result was confusing. The new run information had to be entered into the computer-aided-dispatch (CAD) system manually. This process was going to take a few weeks to implement. In the meantime, we ran calls as dispatched although not logical for our assigned area of responsibility.

We responded to calls as dispatched to cut down on the confusion for the dispatcher and fire units. The battalion chiefs were responsible for completing performance evaluations and station inspections for the new stations, but they didn't run emergency calls with them yet. It was just more confusion that could have been prevented with better planning.

I had started the executive fire officer (EFO) program at the NFA while assigned to fire training and completed it. It required I attend the academy for two weeks every year for four years, and then I completed research and submitted an applied research project (ARP) within six months of the completion of the class. The class itself narrows the topics of what the ARP can be written about. It was something the department embraced when our prior fire chief became the fire administrator. It was required to be eligible to compete for promotion to the rank of district chief.

Secrecy and lack of department input was a continuing trend. I wrote my last EFO paper on the topic of the department's reorganization. For something so secret, the information was available to complete an entire report. It is designed to allow the fire chief of a department to assign the candidate a topic that is of concern to the department. Then the chief followed the progress of the research. No one encouraged me to attend, although it was a requirement for chief officers.

The certification was presented at a special conference your department sent you to upon completion. The fire chief made a presentation during the following monthly staff meeting in front of all the other chiefs. A flag was flown over the capitol and given to you. My flag was delivered by a fellow battalion chief on my shift in the kitchen of a fire station.

I had to inquire about the status of my EFO certificate. It had been received and forgotten in the fire administration office. No one had sent me to the national presentation to receive it or had any intention of presenting it to me at the monthly staff meeting. It had been sitting in the corner on the floor in one of the chief's office for several months. The fire academy sent the certificate to your department's fire chief.

My transfer out of the slow battalion put me back in the marine division. Part of the reorganization was that there would be an administrative chief over that division. The outline of what their duties were hadn't been determined yet.

Because the reorganization had been such a secret, the marine crews in the station were unsure who to go to for operational and maintenance issues. The new marine division chief was contacted. He had no background in marine operations. He hadn't been given any direction so he was unsure how to handle operations in the marine division.

It seemed logical for me to handle day-to-day marine equipment maintenance issues. If there were reoccurring problems with marine resources, he could follow up. The marine calls were something the battalion chief on duty would run.

The marine training topics would be his responsibility. The scheduling of the units for training would occur at the battalion level. They required a backfill unit to cover marine units out doing training. We made an agreement to run operations this way until more information was available.

The marine division had always been the last priority of the three special-operations divisions. The hazmat division had state funding to support their operations. The fire chief was partial to the technical rescue and FEMA divisions and ensured they received any available funding.

Most of the marine resources were obtained secondhand or through the regional marine incident response team (MIRT). A retired member of the department was the MIRT manager. He provided grant money to support our cities marine division due to lack of support. Because there was a lack of commitment to the marine division, the commitment of personnel was lacking.

The chiefs responsible for the marine division were temporary, and this added to the lack of progression of the division. Marine policies were requested by senior staff. Before they would approve any operational marine policy, they did a thorough investigation. Questions were answered, but before any decisions could be made new transfers of chiefs would occur. This pattern kept repeating itself. Work would be repeated, but no working marine operations document was ever produced.

During my first assignment in the marine division, I provided input and work that was completed on the document. I encountered the same roadblocks years later—no progress had been made on the project since the last time I worked on it. Years later, the document still hadn't been approved.

It was frustrating for marine team members. Progress was slow. Many of the boats were acquired through military surplus. Some of the acquisitions origins were questionable. The acquired resource was inventoried to the department. Then new replacement equipment was requested.

The technical-rescue company started by the early members of the technical-rescue team branched out to include marine resources. They tried to expand their training to swift-water rescue operations. The private company that taught special operations purchased some of the same military boats acquired by the city. They owned a trailer that could carry two of the marine Zodiac boats. They provided their trailer to pull the city's marine Zodiacs.

Their trailer was fitted for a tow package by the city garage. The coordinator at the city garage arranged for a tow package from a private dealership not under the city contract to do the work. The package he selected did not match the city trucks that would tow the trailer. The trailer did not allow the motors to be on the Zodiacs if stacked on top of each other.

The technical-rescue team got involved with marine operations by providing necessary resources for the marine division to use to continue their operations. This allowed for a friendly transition when they got into the swift-water rescue business.

The deputy chief who arranged the acquisition of the Zodiacs was involved in the private business that taught technical rescue. It was a conflict of interest. Members of the marine division were uncomfortable with the parameters of using private, non-city-owned equipment and with the acquisition of the private equipment and its use.

They didn't feel comfortable operating their equipment and were unsure of the consequences if the equipment was damaged during its use. Issues were ongoing. Coming back to the marine division revealed many of the same issues were unresolved. The same obstacles were present in the marine division during my absence.

The marine equipment acquisition and training for the technical-rescue team had been supported by senior staff because their loyalty was to the technical-rescue division.

During holidays in the summer, the fireboats were staffed full time. Normally, they responded from the station if they received a marine call. During the summer, there is higher water traffic. The overtime and backfill for the station was not arranged for the next holiday.

A large residential fire occurred in the marine station's first-run response area. The remaining truck in the station was on a rescue call. The closest ladder trucks weren't available for the call. The first ladder on scene responded from a great distance. It was a large defensive fire that required the use of a ladder pipe. Senior staff had got caught playing the odds that the marine station wouldn't get a call while the fireboat was staffed for the holiday.

The battle over whether the marine station should be backfilled for holidays had been a debate that went back and forth over several years. No definitive answer was ever made. Each holiday, the subject reappeared for debate.

The chief put a higher importance on the technical-rescue team in the department, even though they ran the least calls. That team was given priority over all other programs in the department.

Another administrative frustration after my transfer back to the busy battalion involved one of the captains in my battalion who got a DUI charge. He had to resign or be fired. No matter how many times it happened to other firefighters, it continued to occur.

It was ironic that while in training, there were only a few integrity connection instructors for the city. The position to teach integrity connection was part of my duties for my assignment to the training center. The fire department was one of the first departments to have all their members complete the class.

The program was designed by the city audit department. There were few members in the city that were certified to teach the class, so as an instructor you taught classes to other departments in the city. The goal was to gain instructors within each department so they could teach their own classes in the future.

The instructor pool stayed small, so routinely classes were taught with a mix of other city departments. What other departments in the city thought about the fire department surprised me. They didn't think the fire department had integrity. I had found it to be true, but it was surprising to hear it recognized outside the department.

It was routine for senior staff, when guilty, to be the first ones to announce their displeasure with a practice. It was their strategy to distance themselves from the issue.

Senior department leaders were among some of the first to take a lead position to teach integrity connection. They lacked integrity, but they wanted to be the first to embrace its importance. It hadn't fooled anyone. Other departments that interacted with them saw through the tactic.

They provided examples during the class to confirm their opinions. They voiced their displeasure at how command vehicles were allowed to have tinted windows, although a violation of state code. Particularly concerning to waste management was how firefighters were allowed to go to funerals of members on duty because they had to take leave.

Mustaches and personal appearance were part of their concern. The mustaches they saw were not groomed, and they asked if we didn't have policy to regulate the length. They pointed out the fire chief himself had the longest mustache. Just by the appearance of our chiefs, they had an immediate dislike and distrust of them. When I asked them how they made those assumptions, they said it was the way the chiefs conducted themselves and treated others as if the chiefs were better than others were.

Some complained that they had applied for jobs with the fire department and had not even gotten an interview, but children of high-ranking officers had. No one ever knows the entire reason people make the decisions they do, but a strong leader is able to withstand close scrutiny.

A lot of unethical practices within the fire department were easy for senior staff to explain, and you were punished if the subject was brought up. There was always a rehearsed explanation for their actions. It looked suspicious because of the number of chief's sons who were hired above thousands of other applicants.

Some of the animosity between departments was real, and some had to do with perception. My last shift, the rescue department complained against one of my crews. The fire crew had run eight rescue calls that night between the hours of midnight and four in the morning. The rescue crew had made a complaint to their supervisor who became involved and wanted to meet with the crew.

The main basis of the complaint was that the fire crew was mean to the ALS provider who'd arrived several minutes after the fire crew had been on the scene. The call was for a breathing difficulty. Upon arrival, the fire crew found the patient stable and breath sounds clear.

During the short time on scene, they communicated the initial patient status, but simultaneously upon the other ALS provider's arrival on scene, the patient started experiencing pain upon inhalation. This changed the patient's treatment. The rescue crew initially had gone to the wrong address. The fire captain had seen them and corrected them on the radio. The ALS provider had taken this direction to be offensive. When the rescue crew had gotten to the door, the fire captain had directed them to bring in the stretcher and the drug box.

When they had gotten to the door, the fire captain had told them to turn the stretcher around because the hallway had been narrow and the stretcher wouldn't have been able to be turned around in the room.

Since the condition of the patient changed, there was more urgency to start an IV. The ALS provider was agitated because they had gone to the wrong address and he was getting updated information as he entered the room. He said he was offended by the directness of the orders given by the fire captain for equipment and stretcher placement. He was offended, so he no longer listened to the patient status given from the fire ALS provider.

The fire crew was confused by his agitation. They weren't aware of doing anything to create his animosity. They thought he was disrespectful for not listening to the patient information, but continued patient care. They had never seen him on any rescue calls. This rescue ALS provider said the fire crew slammed the door when they loaded the patient in the ambulance. The fire crew said they performed the task the same way they had for every other rescue call that day. The doors are heavy and require a harder push to ensure they properly close.

I think this story is an example of how past indiscretions over time skew current perceptions. This EMS call complaint had more to do with misconceptions than it did with actual wrongs done.

Early in my career, fire and rescue shared a building. Rescue had a mentally handicapped person wash their ambulances. There was a lot of animosity then between the fire and rescue departments. The fire department resented the rescue department because they had to run a large number of rescue calls. The rescue department couldn't manage the large call volume. They couldn't keep up with the call demand. The fire department was not given authority then to practice ALS skills off the fire trucks.

The rescue department resented the fact that they had to rely on fire units to cover their rescue calls. The fire department was responding to a majority of the medical calls for the rescue department. A fire unit was dispatched when there wasn't a rescue unit available or because they were closer by time or distance. They frequently got on the scene first.

Since the fire department arrived on scene first, they provided most of the medical care before a rescue unit arrived. In a lot of cases, the rescue unit arrived just to transport the patient to the hospital.

The rescue department controlled who was released to practice as an ALS provider. It is still true today. In the early days, fire personnel were required to run two twelve-hour rescue shifts on their day off without compensation to be able to practice their ALS skills off the fire truck when they were working.

These working conditions caused both departments frustration. The person washing ambulances didn't have animosity toward anyone. He was friendly and kind. His biggest stressors were that the fire department would take over the rescue department, and he would lose his job washing ambulances. Fire crews teased him to get a reaction when they were bored waiting for the next emergency call.

He died around the time of this recent complaint. It was disappointing to realize that some things hadn't changed between the two departments. The progress had been slow. The fire and rescue departments hadn't progressed to the level they should. It had been many years with a lot of calls run between them, but they were still unable to work together.

The same complaints and problems were being discussed. The fire and rescue departments had not overcome these issues or bad feelings. Quality patient care should remain the focus. It was another example of basing decisions on emotions versus practicality.

The mission to provide service to others in a critical time wasn't being fulfilled. Both sides had allowed personal feelings to interfere with what they had sworn to do. The working relationship between the two departments hadn't improved, and neither had the attitudes of the leaders in the organizations.

I could no longer deny, support, or make excuses for senior staff's lack of integrity. They had lost their moral compasses, and it was beyond my ability to change. We differed on what was considered ethical. We didn't share the same values.

The question for me was whether there was still a responsibility to do something about it. My hope had been to be promoted to influence the leadership of the department for good. My love of the fire service drove me to want what was best for it. A few bad officers were ruining the reputation and the internal environment of the fire department.

Leaders have the highest moral obligation to maintain their integrity. Somewhere along the way they had lost it. They had violated their positions and were operating above rules and policy. Their power had given them the attitude that they could do whatever they wanted and not be accountable for their actions.

On my last shift, I ran two calls in the middle of the night. Neither one of them was with the fire companies where the battalion chief slept, which is unusual. One of the calls was dispatched because of the problems with the changes in the reorganization. The other was an upgrade to a fire from a fire alarm because there was a haze of smoke in the building.

I never turned on the emergency lights, and I cleared quickly. The duty district chief responded. He was dispatched because of the type of structure, but the comments of the case gave discretion to just monitor the case on the radio. Instead, he responded with lights and sirens which could be heard over his radio transmission that he was responding.

This district chief only competed with himself for promotion. The qualifications for promotion were written for him. There was only one other person eligible to compete for the promotion. They held the promotional process when the other person eligible was out of town. The process was downgraded to a written question. He just had to put his name on the paper.

The way he made decisions was different than most. He had spent most of his career in an administrative position. When he was a captain, he ordered his driver to respond to a fire alarm in an emergency mode when the emergency lights on the truck didn't work. The driver was uncomfortable doing this. It was against state law. It was an uncomfortable position for me riding in the jump seat on relief.

The likelihood of the incident being an emergency was low based on the dispatcher's comments. Both of us protested. He became angry when challenged. Fortunately, the first fire unit arrived on scene and confirmed that it was a light ballast problem and cleared all other incoming units. We no longer had to respond to the call.

He gave the driver a written reprimand for questioning his order. The driver grieved the discipline because he had only been trying to follow the law. He did not feel safe driving in an emergency mode to the call.

The battalion chief didn't want to give the firefighter a reprimand either. He had prior experience in the safety office and knew the laws. He had knowledge of driving infractions and accidents. He sat on a city panel to decide outcomes for employees involved in vehicle accidents. He knew the firefighter had correctly refused the request and followed state law.

The reprimand was upheld up the chain of command. The battalion chief was given a reprimand for not enforcing the reprimand given by the captain. He was transferred to the slow battalion as further punishment. The chief liked this captain, and he was moved through the ranks quickly.

I didn't know about the firefighter's discipline for quite a while. No one had requested a statement from me about the incident as a witness to the event. That was unusual and against the normal procedure during investigations of incidents. It was unfortunate that the driver had received discipline. Laws had to be broken to comply with the order as well as putting citizens at undue risk while driving without the proper warning devices on the truck. The department acted like they were above the law.

This now district chief continued to use poor judgment and make bad decisions. The driver mentioned in this incident continues to be passed over for promotion without any explainable reason. Senior staff gave input to the fire chief on who should be promoted. He didn't have this district chief's endorsement. This individual was skipped over for promotion because of a driving incident that had occurred many years ago.

Formal discipline was only supposed to stay in an employee's file for eighteen months. The consequences for him have gone on for many years. It is just one of the examples of their selective punishment.

After getting back to the station on my last shift, another call was dispatched for a fire alarm. My unit shouldn't have gotten dispatched to the call, but I responded anyway. The dispatch error was caused by the problems with the reorganization. The station on the call had been moved out of my battalion.

Both calls I ran were in the middle of the night. I made the decision to unmake my bed after the second call and pack my personal belongings and take them to my vehicle. Everything except my personal protective gear was in my car when my relief arrived.

The battalion chiefs have an hour earlier shift change. My crews weren't out of bed yet. I put my gear in my vehicle. I left the station without anyone seeing me leave. I was scheduled to be out on vacation leave for a few weeks. I had accrued so much leave that it had to be used or lost because not all of it could transfer over to the next year and the balance exceeded the amount that could be paid at retirement. I rarely took leave; I was too dedicated to my profession.

My last shift ended. The lights weren't turned on for my last call. The highlight of my last shift was having my vehicle washed.

When I pulled up to one of the stations the day before, crews had proceeded to wash my vehicle. It was significant because it was my last shift. I also noticed it because the crews washing the vehicle were on the technical-rescue-squad truck. Generally, a task like washing a battalion vehicle was completed by one of the newest members of the department. It was a genuine demonstration of respect because of who performed the task.

It was touching to me because even though senior staff didn't respect me, I had earned the respect of the crews I worked with. They were who mattered. They performed the actual job of firefighting. They ran the calls every day. Their earned respect was what really mattered.

The many fires I responded to had not been the real challenge in my career. The physical demands were high, but they weren't unattainable. Some of the people I had to work with had been the real challenge.

Many fires had successfully been extinguished, but this type of fire wasn't capable of being extinguished.

I did not want to be a woman in the fire service. I wanted to be accepted as a member of the fire service.

I was unwanted when I arrived and unnoticed when I left. My strategy of hard work and effort to be accepted had backfired on me.

CHAPTER SIXTEEN

PIA

My experience in the fire service confirmed the necessity and importance of conducting postincident analyses to evaluate what things went well and what didn't. They are helpful in real life. Instead of making the same mistakes repeatedly, all of us can learn from mistakes and make the necessary adjustments to correct them. It also gives us the opportunity to continue to practice those things that do work well in our life professionally, personally and emotionally. More importantly, it identifies those things that don't work well.

My experiences in the fire service helped define who I am as a person. The obstacles that presented themselves were opportunities to develop and grow in integrity and deepen my moral convictions. They provided the opportunity to become secure in my beliefs and embrace moral courage to stand up for what I knew to be right.

A difficulty I experienced while operating the truck one day identified the importance of little things. We arrived on scene to a fully involved car fire. The first step was to pull the tank to pump lever. This tank to pump lever allowed water from the tank to reach the pump. The hose line was in place, and the firefighter was on the nozzle ready for water. No water came out of the hose line when the gate was opened.

I repeated all the steps to ensure everything had been done properly. I felt no resistance when the tank to pump lever was pushed in and pulled back out.

I did a visual check from the top of the truck and realized the pin that held the rod together had fallen out. My arm couldn't reach the rod because it was too far inside the pump panel. The system failed because of the absence of a small pin. That small pin held the necessary tank to pump lever together.

Another fire truck had to be requested. There was five hundred gallons of water in the truck but no way to access it. The water directly from a hydrant and a fire extinguisher were the only resources available. They weren't as effective, but they were the only strategies available.

Strategy

There were several fires in a short time frame that occurred in the same apartment complex. The fire causes varied, but no matter what strategy and tactics were used to attack the fire, the outcome was the same. The entire roof burned off the buildings in every fire. The strategy supported fire extinguishment, but the construction didn't. The tasks required supporting the strategy and tactics were performed, but the building construction was flawed.

The buildings had a common attic. When an apartment caught on fire and went undetected, it quickly got into the attic space and burned the entire roof off. A better building design would have been to install fire walls between each unit to limit fire spread.

No fire strategy could overcome the problems with the construction type. The roof burned off the buildings each time because of a design flaw in the construction.

PIA

I sent an email out to the department announcing my retirement. The subject line was "Seagrave PIA." It was a review of my strategies while navigating through the dangerous environment encountered while working within the fire service. Senior staff was responsible for the construction flaws in the organization that made the environment dangerous. Those few people stopped the progress of the organization and halted its effectiveness.

I used a fire analogy to announce my retirement and evaluate my experience in the fire service. It is a PIA of my frustration of not being able to change perceptions of senior officers in the department. It is an evaluation of the undeserved retaliation which resulted in having to take a defensive strategy.

> We have all been to large working fires. The strategies used aren't all the same. Sometimes the tactics used are topics of discussion. Either way the tasks get done. Sometimes risks are taken depending on the situation found upon arrival, and because of our initial size ups. The risks are weighed against the benefits and degree of safety provided to perform these tasks. Always take the time to do a walk around so you can be aware of all the hazards and perform operations safely. When the fire is out no one wants to go to rehab and start the extensive task of overhaul, even though it is necessary to prevent rekindles.

> I want to thank everyone that responded to my many working incidents. I learned something from each one. It helped me be better prepared for the next call for service that came.

> I will be clearing the scene as of April 1. Thank you for your efficient and professional response to all my calls for service and for making the Department what the Fire Service should stand for.

> All clear, fire is out, available for service.

The large working fires I was referring to weren't all actual fires. Many were the conflicts I experienced while trying to navigate through the fire service. The reference to different strategies used refers to the differences in how I approached problems to how senior staff handled issues.

My tactics were scrutinized because I used different methods to accomplish the same thing. The tasks referred to were the actual things done to complete the tactics and support the strategy.

My size-up was an evaluation of the leadership of the department. The risk-benefit identified the threat to my career. The risk existed because I objected to their strategy and tactics, which weren't safe.

My walk around provided a full picture of what was at stake when objections were made. The walk around identified a risk to the safety of my career.

Rekindled fires that start because not all of the hot embers are extinguished can be more serious than the initial fire. The overhaul of my career had to be completed. The rehab of retirement provided a safe environment in which to do it.

Firefighting is an exciting and rewarding profession. The reference to going to rehab is my resistance to retiring. The hesitancy existed even though it was the safest thing to do.

Thanking everyone for responding to my many working fires was sincere. Without their efforts, my career wouldn't have been successful. Each incident really did provide a learning environment that prepared me for future fires, both on actual fires and within the department.

Clearing the scene was fire terminology used to announce my retirement. I was extending sincere thanks to the firefighters who do the job every day while maintaining their integrity in spite of the environment that may find themselves in while trying to fight their personal fires.

All clear was my farewell. *Fire is out* was my extinguishment of my career with the department. *Available for service* was my desire to continue to serve in some capacity in the fire service. I still want to make it better.

Escape Plan

Adversity made me better and stronger. The process of working through adversity increased my strength and ability to make good decisions. My focused attention built my capacity to get past obstacles and reach my desired goal.

Starting over provides the opportunity to find another means of egress. Obstacles and warning signs were there to stop me in the beginning, but I disregarded them and only saw the obstacles as challenges to overcome no matter what.

I identified my escape plan and had found a way out. It was necessary for me to retreat for my safety and for the safety of others in my crew. My efforts weren't effective, and I found no other option but to retreat.

My fire was out with the department. I could no longer support the chief's philosophy and management strategy. I still love the fire service and what it stands for. I didn't announce my retirement ahead of time because the senior staff was still looking for ways to discipline me. It was a defensive tactic but also an effective strategy.

They had inflicted the most damage to my career. The knowledge that my continued efforts didn't have the ability to change their attitude made any continued attempts unproductive and unnecessary. They had become retaliatory in their actions to quiet my protests to their actions. An escape plan was identified, but it couldn't be shared.

To share the escape plan would block my own egress.

Preplan

I didn't have the necessary water supply to put this fire out. I wasn't ready to turn the hydrant on because the right connection hadn't been made. My boots and surroundings were getting too tight, and I had to cut my losses.

At the time, some of the tasks I performed were tedious, but the rewards came later. The benefit wasn't immediately recognized even though they were a direct result gained from the experience of performing the tasks earlier. These experiences only made me more prepared and better at my job. It paid off for me to take the time to conduct a preplan and strategy.

With preplanning, I sized up the threats ahead of their occurrence and planned my strategy to ensure my personal safety. Anyone can predict obstacles to their safety with a well-prepared plan and strategy that prevents them from reaching their destination or goal.

I became more competent with proper preplanning and having a strategy resulted in having more control over my situation. This competence increased my confidence and soothed my fears in future dangerous situations.

Preplans helped me ensure I was prepared when confronted with making critical decisions.

My annual physical occurred each year on my birthday. The age requirement was met to retire. The office to fill out retirement paperwork was in the same building where the physicals were conducted.

Benchmarks

Every time I was willing to try something new, I gained some knowledge or experience from doing it. Moving to an office job from fire operations broadened my perspective on how the whole fire department ran. It gave me better perspective and allowed me to do a better job for the department.

When back in fire operations, I knew more about fire origin and cause. My perspective was broadened to consider that a fire may be intentionally set. Media influence and working closely with those affected by a fire opened my perspective to department influence.

I evaluated the benchmarks of fire-under-control and fire-out progress reports in my life. It was essential to keep my fires under control. Then after the immediate threat was handled, I could assess how to completely extinguish a fire.

A meeting with an adviser revealed that the benchmark requirements to retire with full benefits had been met. Mental preparation started after the meeting with the deputy chief when he didn't acknowledge my position as a chief officer. That meeting provided evidence that my hard work and effort hadn't produced the desired results.

The realization that my accomplishments hadn't changed the perception of my position in the department established an emotional benchmark. The physical benchmark occurred at the annual physical. These experiences prepared me to retire. The disappointment in my inability to overcome prejudice gave me the resolve to retire.

Not everything in life can be planned.

One fire around Christmas resulted in a fatality. A man, who lived alone, had several inflatables decorating his front yard for the holiday. The decorations were inflated the night of the fire. It made for unusual combination of holiday gladness mixed with fatal dancing flames. He had been at a local bar drinking the night before. His intoxication further altered his consciousness.

He was found in his home in an embarrassing position. He had not planned on having a fire that night.

Another young man had a similar experience. He had been smoking marijuana. The electrical panel was used to turn appliances on in the kitchen. While he was leaning over a stored mattress trying to reach the electrical panel, the marijuana joint he was smoking dropped down on the mattress. The mattress caught on fire.

Instead of calling the fire department, he tried to put the mattress out himself. He thought he had extinguished the mattress, so he fell asleep on the couch. When he woke up, the fire was bigger. He dragged the mattress to the front door and blocked his own way out of the apartment.

Then he went into the bathroom and called the fire department. The dispatcher encouraged him to jump out the bedroom window because he couldn't get out the front door. He thought he would get hurt if he jumped out the window because he lived in a two-story apartment building.

He chose to remain in the apartment. The decision to stay in his apartment cost him his life.

Staying in the fire department would be dangerous. The hazards were known. A means of egress was found and used. I didn't want to be caught in an unplanned emergency scenario.

A man who suffered a house fire was willing to admit he was smoking marijuana before he was willing to tell his wife he was looking at pornography when the fire occurred. The improperly disposed of smoking material had caused the house fire. What he was doing while looking at pornography allowed the fire to go undetected.

I didn't want to be distracted fighting an actual fire and have my career exposed to the certain spread of fire that was growing in intensity.

My Life: The Size-Up

My first size-up of fires was that they were hot and could seriously burn you. There were some intentionally set fires that could still deliver unintended results, just like good intentions can deliver dangerous outcomes.

By conducting routine size-ups I gathered information to develop a strategy. I was open to input received by those performing the tactics that supported the strategy. By doing this I had the information available to make the best decision.

Those performing tasks had information to share to help me develop my overall strategic plan. I tried to keep mental notes and learn something from each incident or experience I encountered. It helped me in the next incident I responded to. It made the difference in my survival. Though the road was hard, I benefited from the experience and grew stronger in my resolve to succeed. I learned something from every challenge I encountered.

Our crew had limited fire tactical knowledge at the time of the recruit fire. Decisions in life can present themselves with the same limited knowledge before you are called to make them. My experience provided me valuable information I was able to use throughout my career. I judged every fire I went on against my recruit fire. I now had firsthand knowledge and a gauge for all other fires I responded to.

I couldn't have gotten this experience any other way. I gained a conviction of the importance of team integrity, a water supply, the need for good communications and dangerous fire conditions I couldn't have received in any other way. The attainment of this knowledge didn't come without a price. It required courage because I had to face fear. I also received some injuries. The consequence was a painful burn.

The realization of how fortunate I was increased as I progressed in my career. Fear can be a good thing. It is a check and balance that forces you to do a size-up and risk-benefit analysis of a situation. While you are presented with overcoming hard dilemmas, you gain experience, and the result is confidence to accomplish them. There is no other way to gain this confidence.

The intensity of the heat from this fire gave me a thermostat to gauge the progression of interior fires throughout my career. I now had a gauge of when fire conditions were rapidly changing and a flashover was imminent. It let me know when to get out and how far I could be inside a structure and still safely perform operations. It also proved to me that dangerous operations require a strong incident command system (ICS).

Your acceptance into a group is not guaranteed. There was adversity to change and allow women in the fire service. My first greeting was not a welcome one. Having statements like deceased fire chiefs rolling over in their grave upon my entering the fire station wasn't the welcome hoped for. Similar challenges exist in life.

Naked firefighters might not be walking around your desk at work, but you still experience distractions to accomplishing your goals. Focus on the goal. Make sure the goals being pursued risks are worth the costs to obtain it. Extreme fire conditions like flashovers are just not tenable.

Most people have experienced feeling like they didn't fit in a group. It may have even been communicated that your presence wasn't appreciated. It happens to almost everyone sometime in their lives, whether it is at school, work, social groups, or even at home. It is hard to feel like you matter when you can't gain the acceptance of your peers.

There are all kinds of marketing techniques that try to convince us we won't be important without a certain someone or something, or that we have to look a certain way. Firefighters sometimes have to decide if the risk to personal safety is worth the benefit. Perform your own size-up and risk-benefit assessment before you proceed.

Our life experiences present choices. Not all choices are easy to make. Not everything about a situation can be controlled. The only thing that I could control was my reaction to it.

I have found that difficulties in life are opportunities to resolve to increase the effort to overcome them. This process built strength to handle future challenges.

There are proven steps to ensure success like pulling a tank to pump lever, but sometimes the lever doesn't function properly. When no water came out when I tried to overcome prejudice, I retraced my steps. I evaluated my strategy to see if I'd missed a step.

I reviewed all the benchmarks and ensured they were all completed. I found the outcome did not have the desired result. The lack of resistance on my lever was an indication my strategy wasn't working.

Parts of my plan fell apart like the pin fell out of the tank to pump lever. My ability to put the plan back together was as difficult as reconnecting a rod that I couldn't reach.

A plan can be thrown off course by just one person. One person in the right position can damage the plan and make it fail. That one person is as important as the pin was to hold a rod together.

Don't stop when one person alters your goals. Alter your strategy to accomplish the goal.

Strategic Plan

The priorities of life should be supported by the strategy used to live your life. Your actions should support what you really want to achieve. Strategies to fight fires use tactics and assigns tasks that fit the overall strategic plan of protecting life and property. Our life strategies should include tactics and tasks to accomplish our strategic life goals. If your strategy is to acquire a good job, then one of your tactics may be to attain an education. The tasks of playing a sport, getting good grades, and taking out student loans support the tactics and overall strategy. The strategy to attain an education helps ensure your professional and occupational success.

I required a strategy from the very beginning to navigate through my fire service career. I had to decide when proposed with the question of whether I wanted to go to the fire academy as a guest and not as a participant what reputation I wanted to have within the fire department.

I wanted to be taken seriously and employed the tactics of hard work and performed the tasks necessary to be considered a member of the department. My strategy was to excel at the tasks necessary to become a good firefighter and not to become a fulfillment of some sort of quota of females in the fire service.

My strategy of hard work and perseverance wasn't flawed, but the people in my organizational department's structure were. No strategic plan could overcome the obstacles presented to a female striving for advancement within my department. No matter what education, training, or experience strategy I used, I couldn't change the outcome. The outcome remained the same, just like the fire strategies used in common attic construction didn't stop the roof from being burned off.

The problem for minorities in today's fire service is the solid perceptions of construction the leaders have about the minorities they manage. There was a construction problem with senior leadership's perception and philosophy.

The size-up identified the problem early, but the progression of the problem was too involved to prevent its damaging effects. The risk exceeded the benefits for me to remain in the fire service, and is probably why there are still few minorities in the fire service today.

Risk-Benefit Analysis

You have to focus on your end goal and evaluate the risk against the benefit of getting there.

The risk I took of operating a fire truck without training outweighed the benefit of gaining the respect of other firefighters. That risk produced little benefit. The risk to personal safety was greater than the benefit of respect that might be gained.

Accept challenges, but identify the limits. Know when something that isn't safe to do or really doesn't hold any benefit in accomplishing it. Sometimes things are too dangerous, and safety is in jeopardy. Limits should be preplanned ahead of time. Decide now what is really important and worth taking the risk for.

My captain's approach to personal safety was not a good influence for a new recruit. Without my recruit experience, his example would have had more influence on me. The bad habit of not wearing PPE could have resulted in injury later in my career.

Before determining and initiating your attack strategy, remember to do a risk-benefit analysis, and evaluate if what you are saving is worth the risk.

The risk to my retirement and the depth of the efforts that senior staff took to retaliate against me were real. I had made many sacrifices for the fire service but grew to love it. My size-up of the hazards of losing my retirement while conducting a risk-benefit analysis showed no possibility of changing my environment. All my hard work and years in the department had not changed the opinions of the men who led it.

The way senior officers managed was not going to change. The benefit to retire before I received discipline outweighed staying in the fire service. The fire department is a life of service. I loved and was dedicated to the fire service, but my commitment wasn't recognized and efforts to be a part of decision making in the organization weren't appreciated.

Offensive versus Defensive

If there is something you personally need to work on to improve your character as a person it may bring the greatest rewards or benefits. If the environment is unsafe or you have to sacrifice personal integrity, it may be safer to perform an exterior defensive attack. You may lack the influence or authority, which may limit your effectiveness, and you can only perform defensive operations.

Whether you initiate an offensive or defensive attack is based on your personal readiness and the benefit to risk performing an interior attack. If the environment is unsafe or you have to sacrifice personal integrity, it may be safer to perform an exterior defensive attack. I lacked enough influence, and it limited my effectiveness.

A fire early in my career taught me the importance of conducting a risk-benefit analysis. The fire occurred in an old house with balloon construction. The fire quickly traveled up through the walls and into the attic. The fire was well involved upon our arrival. The wife was standing outside on the porch section of the roof. Firefighters assisted her down by a ladder. Then they went back up to try to rescue her husband.

During this short time, the fire flashed and blew out all the windows at the same time. One firefighter was on the porch roof and appeared to be engulfed in flames. He jumped off the roof to safety. The husband perished in the fire.

The initial hand line that came off the truck ended up not reaching the house because of the way the house was sitting on the lot and the distance it was from the street. A longer line was requested, but the fire had already progressed and required a bigger and longer line. This hose line was being put together when the fire flashed.

It was now a defensive fire. Master-stream devices were used to protect nearby exposures and to try to extinguish the fire. The fire attack had started out as an interior attempt to perform a fire-victim rescue. The fire quickly progressed and made it necessary to perform a defensive attack.

All efforts to reach the fire victim failed, including a close call with one of the firefighters in his attempt to reach him. The wife shrieked in terror as her home quickly became entirely engulfed in flames and she realized there was no hope to rescue her husband and he had perished in the fire. The fire had progressed too far before our arrival.

Fire Extension

Check for fire extension in hidden places. After a fire is under control, you still have to check the exposures to ensure the fire hasn't traveled. If those hidden places aren't checked for extension, the fire will present itself later even more intensely, as it will have been allowed to progress undetected.

Look for the underlying reasons or places the fire or problem started or progressed to. It will give you an idea of the problems origination or location. You have to assess if you are really all right with an outcome or all right with the job you are asked to do. If you aren't willing to go deeper to find all the places a problem may be hiding, it will only get bigger. Don't just treat the symptoms, but take the time to diagnose the real problem.

This fire example had quickly progressed and had already extended through the walls and into the attic before our arrival. The fire had just not vented through the roof yet.

The attempts of senior staff to retaliate had extended before I was aware of their attempts. Their efforts were too extensive to maintain a safe environment to safely perform my job. Emergency incidents, management decisions within my battalion, and officers working with me were targets of scrutiny in an effort to find cause to discipline me. Efforts were made to discredit me because I had firsthand knowledge of their motivations and knew about some of the poor decisions they made.

Their perceptions were too ingrained to reach the deep-seated depth of where they developed. Their beliefs were automatic parts of who they were. This made it only possible for me to fight this fire defensively.

Many of senior staff's decisions were not supported by the majority of battalion chiefs, but they were still responsible to enforce the direction given by the fire chief.

Inappropriate decisions were filtered to fire operational crews to try to keep morale up and to protect the fire chief.

Battalion chiefs were the middle managers of the department who ensured the fire chiefs directions were followed in fire operations. It was a balancing act between supporting the chain of command and doing the right thing for operational crews.

This buffering is what endeared battalion chiefs to operational crews and could alienate them from the fire chief.

There was a duty to enforce directions given by the fire chief. Those objectives sometimes conflicted with battalion chief's ability to maintain their personal integrity.

Conflicts occurred between being able to serve the public, meeting the needs of operational crews and still being able to fulfill the fire chief's wishes. The struggle was greatest when the fire chief's directions didn't align with my ability to maintain my moral integrity or make it possible to provide for others' needs.

Primary versus Secondary Searches

Conduct a primary search but take the time to do a secondary search for casualties. My initial size-up didn't identify all the hazards. My primary search of issues didn't find the true cause. Eventually my deeper more thorough secondary searches revealed the motivations behind senior staff's decisions.

Rescue efforts were not driven by immediate threats found. Extensive secondary searches revealed personal motivations were the basis on which decisions were made.

The situations found were disappointing. The searches uncovered a deeper motivation that made decisions impossible for me to support. I was presented with a dilemma because I couldn't follow the fire chief's wishes unless I compromised my personal integrity. I couldn't follow some directions without engaging in illegal or immoral behavior.

Since I refused to follow some of the fire chief's wishes, I became the object of retaliation. My refusal to follow unpopular decisions made by the chief and the treatment I received from senior staff because of it endeared me to fire personnel.

The product of my searches identified their motivations. The little things added up to insurmountable things that I couldn't overcome. Every incorrect decision of senior staff led me to make corrections. The gap between the two grew wider. Senior staff's philosophy didn't match mine.

Exposure Control

Exposures have to be controlled both inside and outside the structure on fire, or they can spread to nearby homes or spread inside a home in hidden spaces in the walls and progress to the attic. Critical decisions in life can affect and spread to threaten your personal integrity. Your decisions can extend externally and also affect those around you.

My retirement provided a safe way to end my career on my terms. The full benefits of retirement would be realized. No one else who worked with me would become an exposure. The extension and dangers to others would stop. My strategy to retire would extinguish the fire.

Safety

Identifying safety hazards is the first thing firefighters are trained to look for. There were safety hazards to my career. If you can preplan the threats, you can plan your strategy to ensure your safety.

Even though mental, emotional, and physical preparations had been made to retire, it was still difficult to do. The walk around of the situation during my size-up confirmed it was the right thing to do. The love of the profession of the fire service still made it difficult.

The conditions identified the potential for a flashover.

Flashover

Flashovers are the sudden ignition of gases when heated to their ignition points. They are sudden and violent, but they can be predicted. The sudden rise of heat can help predict flashovers.

Situations in life can quickly get out of control, but just like flashovers, they can be predicted. The likelihood of their occurrence and your ability to identify them can have lasting consequences.

Attempts were made to find reasons to discipline me. The environment was heating up to the point that retaliation was imminent. The intensity of the heat from a flashover could prove dangerous and even fatal. My career started with a flashover and could end with one, if I didn't correctly identify the signs that current conditions supported one.

Additional resources were needed to assist me.

Mayday

Firefighters call Maydays when they are lost, disoriented, trapped, or running low on air and can't exit a structure without assistance. A lot of fire fatalities occur because firefighters delay asking for help. Not doing a realistic assessment of your circumstances will put you in a dangerous position that if not corrected will require outside assistance to remedy.

I was at the point that assistance was required, but there were no available resources to assist me. When there are insufficient resources at your disposal, it is time to retreat and reevaluate the strategy. Exiting a dangerous situation is the best strategy if it gives you the best chance of survival and if the conditions are serious enough to require the need to call for a Mayday.

Firefighters who find their way out have situational awareness. They are aware where they are in a structure. If they can communicate their location, it increases the success of crews locating them.

Being accountable for air in their breathing apparatus ensures there is enough air to exit the building. If they wait too long to try to escape, they can run out of air before exiting the structure.

Maintaining composure is essential so that efforts are focused on viable ways to exit the structure alive. Panic never produces positive results.

I knew where I was and had identified the hazards in the environment. I had resolved to reach the eligibility age to retire. A high degree of proficiency was maintained to perform my job up to the last shift. The plan of how and when to retire helped me maintain control when the situation became dangerous.

My strategic plan ensured a successful retirement. The short description provided by HRs to all the participants not selected for promotion in the district chief's process referenced a lack of strategic vision. My career was strategically planned, but senior staff lacked the awareness to recognize it.

Things are rarely as grave as you let yourself initially believe. People find it's easier to believe the negative and fear the worse. I let myself believe that if I didn't stay in a near-fatal fire that my world would end over the possible failure of a fire recruit academy.

That poor decision in those few minutes almost cost me my life. The risk to stay inside a building with no life hazard far outweighed any benefits. Because of the investment I had already paid, I decided to work toward excelling in the field. I strived to achieve the privilege of becoming accepted in the fire service. Because I gave so much to the fire service, I grew to love it. No matter how much I sacrificed, it didn't love me back. My strategy backfired.

Each decision I made was a conscious choice. Not all events happened by chance. Many outcomes were because of small decisions I made along the way. A lot were countermeasures strategically maneuvered to defend exposures. This preplanned strategy provided a method to fight current fires, as well as ones just smoldering and starting to burn.

I hope this book brings awareness to the potential challenges people face that might not be visible on the surface. Hopefully it is helpful to anyone facing challenges. The book offers practical strategies to help you make the right tactical decisions to support your strategic plan.

Some choices involve a certain level of risk much like setting a fire to fight a fire. Backfires use intentionally set fires to put out fires and are last-resort strategies when every other strategy fails. My years in the fire service didn't have the desired effect. This book is my backfire strategy.

CPSIA information can be obtained
at www.ICGtesting.com
Printed in the USA
BVHW040220110121
597531BV00020B/886